AGILE PROJECT MANAGEMENT

QUICKSTART & MASTERY GUIDES

AGILE PROJECT MANAGEMENT QUICKSTART GUIDE

A SIMPLIFIED BEGINNER'S GUIDE TO AGILE PROJECT MANAGEMENT

&

AGILE PROJECT MANAGEMENT MASTERY

AN ADVANCED GUIDE TO AGILE PROJECT MANAGEMENT

ClydeBank Media LLC
P.O Box 6561
Albany, NY 12206

Printed in the United States of America

ISBN-13 : 978-0-9963667-4-8

AGILE PROJECT MANAGEMENT QUICKSTART GUIDE

A SIMPLIFIED BEGINNER'S GUIDE TO AGILE PROJECT MANAGEMENT

CONTENTS

How To Use This Book

This book is intended as an introduction to the Agile project management system.

Chapter 1 presents an overview of the concept of project management, and illustrates principles that are germane to the entire subject. The emphasis on Agile commences in Chapter 2, with an explanation of its origin. Its basic structure and methodologies are examined in Chapters 3, 4 and 5. The software tools that are used to implement it are introduced in Chapter 6. Practical application of Agile project management is illustrated by case studies in Chapters 7, 8 and 9 while possible issues arising from such application are discussed in Chapter 10. Further reading is listed in Chapter 11.

Those interested in applying Agile to their projects, either as an experiment or on the basis of a more serious recommendation, should remember that the information provided by this text is general in nature and does not constitute specific professional advice or organizational strategy. As a preliminary source of information, however, it should enable the reader to pursue deeper inquiries and ultimately decide on the suitability of the system and the exact variation to apply.

INTRODUCTION

Some activities are only possible to execute successfully if they are associated with more than one person. They are either too extensive in their magnitude or too sophisticated in their nature to permit performance by a single individual. They require too much work or a diversity of expertise that no one person possesses. It is then necessary to approach these activities using a team.

In addition to the overarching aim of satisfying the original objective, any project, whether in commerce or broader society, requires proper planning and execution, so that the available resources of time, money and labor are appropriately utilized. The management of projects in this way is a distinct discipline in the corporate sphere, replete with its various styles and their proponents. One example of an important yet standard project situation is the development of a new product and its introduction to the market. Several factors, such as the budget for design and construction, the time frame available (given the similar simultaneous offerings of competitors or the urgent demand of the target market), and the specifications of the new product need to be accommodated. One methodology of managing such projects is Agile.

The generation and release of new product offerings is a common occurrence in the software industry. This is where Agile originated, but as a management system it can potentially be applied in any industry that allows for the relevance of its methodology. As a relatively newer phenomenon in business management, it merits attention.

This book examines Agile in detail, including its history, its inner techniques, and its implications for those who use it. The book starts with an outline of the importance of project management per se, works through the various aspects of Agile before turning to a discussion of two cases studies of its application in practice, and finishes with criticism that has been directed at the methodology. There is also an overview of the Agile sub-industry that has arisen, in terms of both advisory services and the software tools that its use necessitates.

CHAPTER ONE

Understanding Project Management

The Necessity of Project Management

The need for diverse yet specialized skills, extensive productive hours, or simply the sheer volume of administrative procedure translates into larger labor forces and expanded possibilities through collective effort. In many professional teams, no single person has the entire scope of expertise and available time to perform the required tasks so as to affect the desired outcome.

The term "project management" refers to the process of coordinating and regulating a collective approach to the execution of a task. The project might be long term in nature, such as the construction of a new high-rise building, or it may be more immediate, such as the repair of an important machine. The skills required to achieve the targeted result may be far beyond what one person is capable of acquiring during their education or career, while the amount of work involved might necessitate a considerable level of participation from other people. At the same time, synchronizing the immense operational detail that is associated with some projects is not possible for a sole individual.

Of course, distributing the scope of responsibility involved in a larger project to more than one person attracts its own related difficulties. Any activity that relies on the commitment and effort of more than one person is subject to obstruction through disloyalty, unreliability or the poor coordination of its component events. For this reason, organizations have tried to establish reliable and standard methods to manage and focus projects, in order to attain the requisite level of cooperation and ensure the success of the collective endeavor.

The scale of a project can be immense. For instance, the budgets of national government departments and multinational corporations can run into hundreds of millions of dollars and entail the participation of thousands of employees. The scope of the project's practical consequences can also be enormous. As an example, The Three Gorges Dam in China, which was completed in the early 2000s, is 660 km in length and contains approximately 9 cubic miles of water, weighing 40 billion tons. This mass of water is so substantial that it actually affects the rotation of the earth to a slight yet significant extent, and it has shifted the position of the magnetic poles by nearly an inch. Its hydroelectric installation generates power equivalent to about 20 nuclear power reactors.

No one person could possibly have constructed the dam on his or her own. Such projects are not merely expressions of nationalist sentiment or aimed at exceptional economic reward, they are necessary to provide amenities to the population and enable the economic growth and stability upon which people rely to survive. The coordination of massive collective efforts is not made necessary by inordinate ambition or ideological misapplication; it is essential to the sustainability of modern existence.

Issues in Project Management

There are certain obvious issues that always arise in the management of collective or group initiatives. Getting a number of people to work together on a single enterprise is not the easiest task in business or society. Anyone who has attempted this in the past should be familiar with that notion. Even a simple activity, such as a sports team or litter-reduction campaign, can be obstructed or delayed to the point that they never materialize.

The first and most basic matter of contention is the reliable participation of everyone in the group. This is harder to ensure in nonprofessional situations. The employment environment usually translates into a more committed attitude from participants, even if they are not entirely dedicated to their jobs or they do not regard their employment as an area requiring more than the minimum of enthusiasm. However, where there is no compensation attached to the project, or where there are no penalties for abandonment of the assigned task, loyalty can be extremely hard to secure. This is seen even in cases where significant monetary reward was associated with participation, such as famous music bands that fell apart.

Once the group has been identified and their commitment to the common task has been confirmed, the issue of sustained and effective communication becomes apparent. This is particularly so in multinational projects, where participants may never have met in person and cannot afford to congregate in the same geographical location. Modern technology has reduced the challenge presented by this situation, but communication within the team is sometimes still an obstacle to its success, even where all of its members are based in the same office. It has already been mentioned that one of the primary reasons for using a group approach is to ensure that all the necessary skills are available. The coordination of these skills then becomes a priority for the project manager. Some of them may only be necessary for a short time, while others need to be available for the entire duration of the project and its aftermath. The proliferation and advanced specialization of skills in some disciplines has resulted in a scarcity of qualified people in certain areas. The effective acquisition and direction of these skills is an important role of the project management strategy.

On a practical level, there are also issues to be negotiated. One assumption about group activities is that they cost more money and take more time. This is not automatically the case, but the management of the project needs to be able to counter or eliminate these eventualities. This is especially so where the project has been initiated in a commercial sphere and has a budget and time-frame approved by a paying customer. It may be a source of extreme disappointment if either of these parameters is exceeded.

Lastly, the customer, the end-user, or even the project participants themselves, need to be satisfied with the outcome. The collective activity must actually produce the intended result. The measurement of this standard is a source of potential conflict. A long-term and expensive project may result in failure. This may not even be due to any fault of the project team, since varying requirements or changing market conditions can cause the customer to adapt their expectations during the course of the project's duration. This final issue, in particular, is addressed by the Agile methodologies. As the Agile management paradigm is discussed in the next chapters, it is important to remember the issues that have been raised in this section, so as to observe how Agile addresses and solves them.

CHAPTER TWO

A History of Agile Project Management

The Agile Alliance

The concept of a standardized or prescribed strategy towards project management is not new. Different organizations or cultures may have practiced their own methods in regulating large labor forces or assigning resources to the projects in which they engaged. However, it was only since the middle of the 1950s that the concept began to be regarded as a more formal discipline and attract its official terminology. At present, it is taken seriously in commerce and elsewhere, as evidenced by, for example, the Association of Project Management (APM) in the UK or the American Society for the Advancement of Project Management (ASAPM). To the extent that project management methods already existed by the turn of the 21st century, Agile Project Management is based on, or a response to, several these preexisting methodologies. Therefore, the formulation and subsequent promotion of a discrete and self-contained management methodology is not a novelty, nor is it surprising that it draws on existing systems of both project and business management.

Agile Project Management (or Agile for short) was devised within the software industry. The process of inventing new software is known specifically as "development". The initiators of the Agile doctrine were all software developers. This is possibly why it has such a strong association with the IT sector. Proponents have made the assertion that it is applicable to any industry, and there is literature examining how this has happened in practice. Its potential deployment in activities outside of IT will be discussed in later chapters of this book.

In early 2000, correspondence about project management techniques was started between the eventual Agile role players. This initial interest blossomed into a formal conference in Chicago in 2001. There, 17 professionals in the software industry hashed out a new method, based on their experience with their respective, preferred alternatives. At this meeting, they composed the various statements that have become synonymous with the Agile movement.

First, they identified what are regarded as the three erroneous assumptions in project management:

1. *It is possible to plan a large project.*
2. *It is possible to protect against late changes.*
3. *It makes sense to lock in big projects early.*

As you can see, these three issues all highlight the point raised at the end of the previous chapter: that the objective of a project (or the end-user's expectations) can change during the course of its execution and make it impossible for the project team to provide a satisfactory result. The first assumption on the list is an allusion to the immensity of some projects and how they are not amenable to a rigid and detailed frame-work or forecasting. Even a simple job like painting a house depends on stable weather. How much more so, then, the construction of a dam spanning an entire mountain range?

The unpredictable nature of the project environment is also encompassed by the four primary principles that the meeting ascertained. These are:

INDIVIDUALS & INTERACTIONS	*over*	PROCESSES & TOOLS
WORKING SOFTWARE	*over*	COMPREHENSIVE DOCUMENTATION
CUSTOMER COLLABORATION	*over*	CONTRACT NEGOTIATION
RESPONDING TO CHANGE	*over*	FOLLOWING A PLAN

Keeping in mind that, while there is value in the items on the right-hand side of the above principles, we value the items on the left side more. The last item is particularly of note here, but the others also serve to illustrate the emphasis on people instead of procedure (the first item), on the efficacy of the end result rather than the bureaucratic administration of its development and presence in the market (the second item), and on customer service and satisfaction over impersonal, disinterested business practice (item three). It should be stated that the emphasis on reducing the administration associated with a project (its bureaucracy or "comprehensive documentation") sometimes attracts the adjective "lightweight" in the context of Agile (as opposed to the "heavyweight" systems that encompass extensive administration and management structures).In trying to establish these principles as the elements of a project management strategy in practice, the meeting generated the following.

12 Principles of Agile Software :

1. *Our highest priority is to satisfy the customer through early and continuous delivery of valuable software.*

2. *Welcome changing requirements, even late in development.*

3. *Deliver working software frequently, from a couple of weeks to a couple of months, with a preference to the shorter timescale.*

4. *Business people and developers must work together daily throughout the project.*

5. *Build projects around motivated individuals. Give them the environment, support, and trust they need.*

6. *The most efficient and effective method of conveying information to and within a development team is face-to-face conversation.*

7. *Working software is the primary measure of progress.*

8. *Agile processes promote sustainable development. The sponsors, developers, and users should be able to maintain a constant pace indefinitely.*

9. *Continuous attention to technical excellence and good design enhances agility.*

10. *Simplicity – the art of maximizing the amount of work not done – is essential.*

11. *The best architectures, requirements, and designs emerge from self-organizing teams.*

12. *At regular intervals, the team reflects on how to become more effective, then tunes and adjusts its behavior accordingly.*

This list of principles is known in the industry as the Agile Manifesto, which consists of the original 17 members who drafted it. They are:

Kent Beck
Mike Beedle
Arie van Bennekum
Alistair Cockburn
Ward Cunningham
Martin Fowler
James Grenning
Jim Highsmith
Andrew Hunt
Ron Jeffries
Jon Kern
Brian Marick
Robert C. Martin
Steve Mellor
Ken Schwaber
Jeff Sutherland
Dave Thomas

There is no need to enter into a detailed analysis of these individuals or their careers in the IT industry. What is important to note is that some of them represented the most prominent existing management paradigms at the time. These were Extreme Programming, Adaptive Software Development, Feature-Driven Development, Pragmatic Programming, Crystal, SCRUM, and DSDM. Some of these are either closely associated with Agile or are regarded as its subsidiary methodologies. What is also obvious from the members' names is that they are related to software development.

One contributor who does merit individual mention is Jim Highsmith, who has gone on to create a reputation for himself as the leading authority on the Agile Project Management methodology. Others, such as Kent Beck and Alistair Cockburn, formulated Extreme Programming (XP) and Crystal methodology, respectively

Motivation

The desire to establish a new, more effective or otherwise improved project management system in the software industry was based on advertised and substantial dissatisfaction with existing methods. This was perhaps due to the expansion of the IT industry, both in terms of its scale and range of application, or merely because the nature of its product makes it the territory for this type of experimentation.

By the year 2000, the Internet, software and computer technology in general were regarded as the machinery of the future, the equipment that would take not only local industries, but the developing global economy, into the next century. People may not remember the Y2K crisis or how excited economists and other commercial observers became with the introduction of IT into each new sphere of economic activity. But the overarching sentiment of the time was one of expectation, complete with all the sci-fi style imaginative prediction that goes with it.

With the IT industry being required to supply solutions on such a massive scale to so many different markets, a refined or even entirely new management approach was a priority, especially one which is so uniquely suited to the industry itself. As an example, Windows 95, an earlier Microsoft operating system (which some younger readers may have to Google to identify), sold 40 million copies in its first year. Microsoft's latest offering, Windows 8, reached 100 million copies in its first six months. One fundamental characteristic of software and its development that may make it susceptible to trouble is what the industry terms "uncertainty." This is more in connection with the already outlined unstable nature of a project and its targeted results. The development of new software is uncertain in that its ultimate desired functionality cannot be determined until it is in use by the customer.

Sometimes, the end-user's expectations change once the software is in use, since they may realize new possibilities or receive more decisive feedback from their own target market. In this way, the software developer is tasked with creating a product that is satisfactory, but simultaneously has to subscribe to the potentially shifting requirements of its commissioner. This is known as "scope creep," and the opportunity that it presents for failure, frustration or miscommunication is obvious.

Prior to the advent of Agile, other management protocols revolved around two basic approaches: Waterfall and Spiral.

Waterfall

Waterfall is the protocol most popularly mentioned in conjunction with Agile and is either seen as an opposing methodology or somehow inferior. It involves developing the software according to a prior plan or determined framework of activity, like the stages in the rapids of a waterfall. It is sometimes referred to as "plan-driven."

Spiral

Also referred to as rapid prototyping, and evolutionary or incremental delivery; these entail the production of pieces of the ultimate product, for the customer to experiment with and provide a response to. They are sometimes described as "agile," i.e., as opposed to the execution of a premeditated plan.

The incremental or phased nature of the second approach seems more compatible with the development of software, since it serves to lessen or even alleviate the uncertainty that is sometimes innate to the process. (For a more comprehensive comparison of Waterfall to Agile, see Chapter 9. This distinction is critical in understanding how organizations go about choosing which approach to use.) In assessing the various sub-methodologies that have arisen under the Agile umbrella, it is important to remember what preceded it and how they have contributed to its present structure and application.

CHAPTER THREE

Basic Strategy

Ag·ile *(adj)* : Able to move quickly and easily

General Outline

Agile Project Management, as the name suggests, is a more rapid or responsive method of process management. Its leading proponent, Jim Highsmith, has written that it enables a much faster, more flexible response to changing market circumstances and the sudden, unexpected tactics of competitors. That is, essentially, how it has come to have the adjective as its official name – due to the supposedly malleable and reflexive nature of the processes to which it is applied.

For this propensity, agile relies on the phased or staged process structure that it represents. Instead of the more traditional Waterfall approach, whereby the project is defined, its parameters stated, and then its constituent steps taken, Agile allows for self-terminating phases or increments. At the end of each phase or "iteration," the customer is presented with a usable product and their feedback is sought in order to modify the next increment. This incremental or iterative approach eventually arrives at the final product or ultimate result.

It should be apparent from this description that Agile makes an adapted end result possible. During the project, the customer or end-user can assist in determining its course, by supplying additional information or changing their expectations entirely. A more rigid approach would merely lead to the delivery of something that the customer would not accept and for which they have little or no use. This might sound like a totally avoidable outcome, but it is notorious in the industry and not limited to smaller projects exclusively.

A suitable metaphor for the Agile system is baseball. The batter represents the project team. The pitcher is the customer. The pitcher/customer explains to the batter what type of ball he is going to pitch, and the batter/team then plans his swing and hopefully makes contact. If everything remains exactly as anticipated, and if the pitcher actually pitches what he said he was going to, the hit is a success. That, in brief, is the Waterfall approach.

However, that is not always what actually happens in baseball or in business. No batter ever knows exactly what the pitcher is going to do. At the same time, outside conditions such as wind, which neither party can control, can affect the trajectory of the ball. In fact, one of the most basic pieces of advice that young batters should be given is, "never premeditate your hit." Agile is, therefore, more closely analogous than other systems, since it allows for adjustment and accommodation during the hit (or project), based on what the pitcher (customer) does and other circumstances in the industry or market environment.

Another metaphor would be the strategy that some immigrants to the United States used during the 20th century to build their homes. Once they had saved enough money to buy a plot of land, they would construct only the basement on the land. That would then be their residence until such time as they had accumulated the financial resources to add one or two stories. This is similar to the Agile system in that the customer (homeowner) is presented with a finished and workable stage of the product at the end of each iteration. If their funds are exhausted or if they realize that they no longer require further development, they can terminate the process entirely. It is somewhat ironic to the metaphor of the unfinished house that, in Agile, the stages are sometimes referred to as "vertical slices."

Basic Strategy

The most important steps in the project management system prescribed by Agile are adapted from a more traditional paradigm. Previously, project management terminology included 5 steps in the process. Highsmith invented his own 5 steps as analogous to those and in accordance with the underlying philosophy of his own system.

They are:

WATERFALL	AGILE
Initiating	Envisioning
Planning	Speculating
Executing	Exploring
Controlling	Adapting
Closing	Closing

The Initiating and Planning stages in the traditional Waterfall process involve identifying what the customer wants and then planning how to provide it, which happens during the Execution stage. Agile, on the other hand, uses the looser terms of Envisioning and Speculating to describe the first two stages, and then Exploring to refer to the actual implementation of the plan. This is because in Agile, the execution of that specific increment does not represent the sole or entire execution phase of the project and, generally, the project is not subject to a fixed product description. Customer feedback is sought and applied to the next Exploring phase. This means that the product is Adapted instead of Controlled. The rigid and narrow philosophy behind the traditional management system is replaced by the more flexible, responsive attitude of Agile.

In assessing Agile, it is important to remember that the system was devised in order to improve the development of new software. That is to say, it is focused on the development of new products, regardless of the industry in which they are used. This may be why Highsmith describes the following 5 main imperatives for the system's application:

CONTINUOUS INNOVATION
Staying current with the customer's needs

PRODUCT ADAPTABILITY
Anticipating the customer's future needs

REDUCED DELIVERY SCHEDULES
Matching supply with changing market demand

ADAPTABILITY
People and processes match market pace

RELIABLE RESULTS
Reduce variation and improve forcasting

These are based on the 4 primary principles in the Agile Manifesto, which are stated in the previous chapter. In general, Highsmith emphasizes the instability of the business environment and assigns more importance to the concrete success of a project than its administration.

Agile is referred to as iterative because it involves an itinerant (phased) process with which to fulfill the customer's needs. It is incremental because it does so in stages of completion. The priority is to produce something at the end of each stage that the customer can use.

Scope & Staff

In keeping with its emphasis on an unknown or unpredictable project outcome, Agile does not specify the final product, as the plan-driven or Waterfall methods do. In the latter, the product or outcome (the scope) of the project is the first item of interest. Estimates are then made as to the entire cost and time-frame of the project. Often, budgets are overrun and additional time is required.

Agile, however, does not specify an exact scope (as is seen in the strikingly inexact terms used to describe its initial steps – Envisioning,

Speculating, or even Exploring to refer to its execution). Rather, its focus is on the available resources of time and money. In this way, the project cannot exceed those parameters. Also, as an iterative process, it allows the customer to terminate their involvement at the end of any iteration, leaving them with a usable product, even if it is not the entire or ultimate output that they initially desired. It is, therefore, theoretically impossible for an Agile project to surpass the available capital investment or its deadline. This approach also has implications for how staff participation in the project is managed. Agile does not tolerate the more traditional top-down (vertical) power dynamic in the management of the project team. Instead, the team members are encouraged to take ownership of the project and manage themselves to a large extent. The Project Manager is merely present to negotiate or remove institutional obstructions and maintain an environment that is conducive to the team's work and success.

All of these factors will become more apparent in the next chapters, in which different sub-methodologies are discussed and case studies are analyzed.

CHAPTER FOUR

Agile Specific Methodologies

The Different Variations of Agile

As stated in the preceding chapter, there are different sub-approaches within the Agile system. These are either derived from theories that existed before the Agile system was officially initiated, or they are the work of individual proponents. Some of them may, therefore, resemble earlier project management paradigms. This hereditary succession or adaptation is not a new phenomenon in project or business management, where there has traditionally been a substantial degree of intermixing and synthetic progression. This chapter does not purport to be an exhaustive discussion of all the available approaches under the Agile heading. These sub-approaches are sometimes referred to as "flavors", a term taken from the software programming environment. The term is an indication of the existing program distinctions to meet variable needs. For example, users who rely on different operating systems.

Trying to assess which approach will suit an organization requires that the project manager is aware of the project's application in practice as well as the nature of the proposed project. Research into the issue is necessary. No matter how positive other people's remarks may be about a specific variation of Agile, each project facilitator needs to contrast it with their situation in order to determine whether it is a suitable course of action.

This list presents 5 of the most important variations in use today. They are not listed in order of importance or prevalence of use. Project managers are advised to observe described principles and established practice, in order to evaluate each approach in relation to their common tasks. Ultimately, no project is ever any more successful than the commitment, hard work, and expertise of its team.

Scrum

Usually, this is the method that the literature on Agile mentions. As an illustration of how Agile operates, it is perhaps one of the best examples to highlight. Its internal processes, terminology and style of team management are an accurate and transparent demonstration of how Agile functions and the philosophy that it entails. One of the first proponents of Agile, Ken Schwaber, was involved in the initial formulation of the Scrum method.

The word "scrum" is taken from the sport of rugby. For those who are unfamiliar with this sport, it is played by 15 players on each side and closely resembles American football. The scrum is a movement that is engaged in by both teams, during which eight players on each side (the heaviest, most physically imposing members) pack together and push against their opponents in a collective effort. But scrum isn't the only piece of rugby terminology in the system. There is also the "kick-off meeting" (which is rather self-explanatory), during which the project is discussed for the first time by the project team, in order to ascertain what the goals are and how they are going to be achieved. During this meeting, the "project backlog" is determined. This is the term used to describe the work that needs to be done, or essentially what the customer desires from the initiative (the scope). The customer is defined, and their requested product is identified to enable the ultimate objective. For example, the 20th century immigrants mentioned in the previous chapter, who want to establish a residential structure, would be the customers. This is known as the user story, or the customer situation, and its use is to determine what work is required and why.

The iterations (stages) within the project are known as its "sprints."

In each sprint, there are backlog items. In keeping with the example of the newly constructed immigrant's home, the first iteration would possibly involve the following items:

- *Excavate the area for the basement and foundations.*
- *Throw the foundations with concrete.*
- *Perform the masonry to construct the walls of the basement.*
- *Lay the slab of the house (the roof of the basement).*
- *Install the piping for plumbing and power.*

Once these items have been completed, the finished stage of the project can be presented to the customer for their assessment and, importantly, their feedback. What is critical to realize about this example is that the homeowner can decide to change their original plans for the house once the basement has been built, because the work stops there temporarily. If they do not have enough money or time to continue with the construction, they are not under any obligation to do so. It may be said that Agile, if successful, is more likely than other project management approaches to result in a win-win situation, or one in which everyone scores. A sprint or "iteration" should not last more than 4 weeks. Sometimes, it may be as short as 1 week. This is another indication of how Agile reduces a project to much smaller, more immediately manageable segments. Yet they are also self-fulfilled phases, giving the end-user something of value, even if it does not represent the entirety of the ultimate desired outcome.

At the start of each Sprint, team members hold a "sprint-planning meeting." If this is not the first sprint, the meeting will be combined with a "sprint review meeting," which focuses on the preceding sprint. The targeted outcome for that particular sprint, the Sprint Goal, is established during this meeting.

At the start of each day, there is also a 15 minute daily Standup

Meeting. The members are required to remain standing for its duration. This is supposed to symbolize and engender the sense of immediacy, alertness and quick response that the system incorporates. In Scrum, this meeting is known as the Daily Scrum, and it is used to plan the next 24 hours of activity. During the Scrum, the following questions have to be answered:

- *What did I do yesterday that was material to the Sprint Goal?*
- *What am I going to do today that is material to the Sprint Goal?*
- *Is there anything stopping us from reaching the Sprint Goal?*

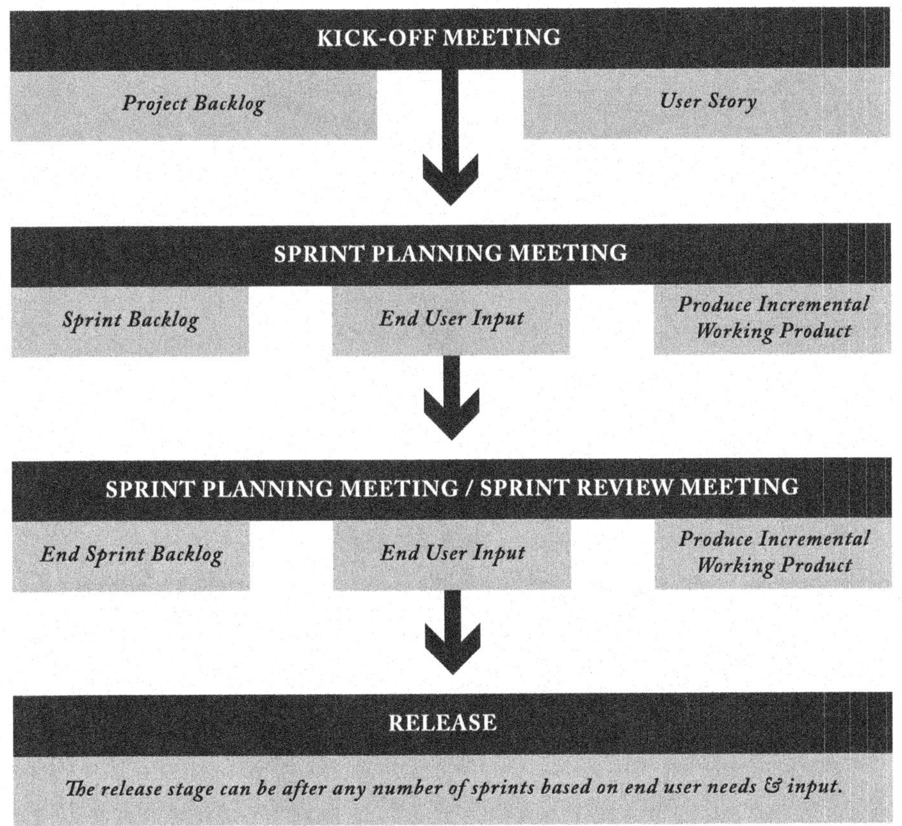

The backlog concept can be applied to either the Sprint or the

Release, which is the eventual delivery of the ultimate product. During the course of the project or sprint, a Burndown Chart is used to track progress at each level. This is a graph that descends in its trajectory, marking project or sprint progress as proportional to the passage of time. The Task Board is used to promote awareness of the project in its entirety, from the user stories through the iterations to the finished stages. It is an invaluable tool for the project team that organizes and tracks tasks that have been initiated, are in progress, and have been completed.

SAMPLE BURNDOWN CHART

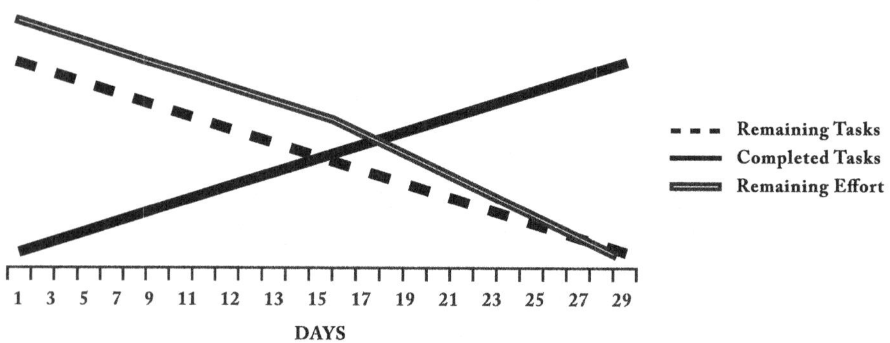

SAMPLE TASK BOARD

STORY	NOT STARTED	STARTED	IN PROGRESS	DONE
USER STORY 1	H	F	B	A
	I	G	D	C
USER STORY 2	J		E	
	K			

In conjunction with the burndown chart and the user story, the task board provides a "one stop shop" of vital information for the Scrum project team. The team in a Scrum project consists of three roles; Product Owner, Scrum Master, and Development Team members.

Product Owner

The Product Owner is the manager of the process. However, they do not micro-manage the people who work on the project. The workers are left largely to manage themselves. Instead, the Product Owner takes responsibility for the list of Backlog items, making sure that everyone knows what is on it and what each item represents. Sometimes, they partially delegate this function to the Development Team. It is important to note that the Product Owner is a single person, not a management team.

Scrum Master

The Scrum Master is the person whose role is devoted to the implementation of the project management system itself. They need to be well acquainted with the Scrum (Agile) paradigm and also be able to convey its practice and ideology to other staff members. They liaise with both the Product Owner and the Development Team in order to ensure that the Scrum system operates as it should.

Development Team

The Development Team is typically small, although preferably not fewer than 3 members. It has no internal hierarchy or titles, other than Developer. It is self-managing, i.e., no other person provides instructions on how to meet the Backlog objectives. The Team comprises all the necessary expertise, and it accomplishes the required level and nature of activity each day. It is, therefore cross-functional.

The output of the Scrum process, such as the Backlog list and the product increments, are known as its artifacts. This discussion of Scrum reveals certain terms and principles that are generic to all of the Agile sub-approaches. In the descriptions that follow, the reader can simply refer back to this definition of Scrum in order to compare and understand them, even though the terms and the internal procedures used in each methodology may not be the same.

Lean

Lean is a business management philosophy employed and made prominent by the Toyota Motor Corporation. It is sometimes referred to as Toyotism or the Toyota Production System. Since the process must take place as quickly as possible, its priority is to ensure that the entire manufacturing process, from the supplier network to the end-user, entails no wasted resources or time. It is an organizational strategy that aims at minimum expense and shortest possible duration with high levels of customer satisfaction.

Applying Lean to Agile is a natural management progression in enterprises that already make use of the former. It is an interesting approach, and it has some apparent advantages and snags. On the plus side, the use of cross-functional teams enables less outlay of expertise. This is seen as a form of waste in the Lean and Six Sigma management paradigms, so the more fully staff is utilized, the better. Because Lean minimizes the costs of the project, it also allows for a greater return on investment (ROI), or a more substantial output on the customer's available budget. On the other hand, Lean also requires constant monitoring of the project. It is sometimes based on statistical or other methods of assessment, and this necessitates the absorption of productivity time by what is essentially an administrative function. Project managers will need to decide whether the reduced expenses occasioned by the implementation of Lean are justified by the additional burden of work that it entails. This coupled with the statistical analysis foundation of Lean makes the pairing of Lean and Agile inappropriate for many product development projects. Lean is best applied to continuous processes (manufacturing or otherwise) while Agile harnesses the incremental production method to produce customer-tailored results.

Crystal

Crystal is another sub-approach that was devised by one of the original 17 composers of the Agile philosophy, Alistair Cockburn. Cockburn still maintains a site on the methodology, and he states that the following three underlying principles in his approach to software development (or any other project):

- *Human-powered* : Maximizing the potential of each person on the project team (people-centric as opposed to other-centric).

- *Ultralight* : The least possible administration and auxiliary activities, regardless of project size or scope.

- *Stretch-to-fit* : Always start out with a little less than you need and expand it to requirements.

These principles reflect the Agile Manifesto (see Chapter 2), and in the case of the third principle, also a Lean aspect. It is no surprise that Cockburn lists reading matter on the Japanese Just-In-Time (JIT) business management system on his site too.

Crystal is not one specific methodology, but rather a "family" or group of business methods. This is a source of criticism, since many methods are not mutually interchangeable and cannot be switched during the course of a project. While Crystal places a strong priority on the testing of the product under development (something which has always been a part of software design), it is not always feasible to have a team member dedicated to that activity in every team. In fact, this requirement may start to breach the second, "ultralight," principle. One of the primary focuses of the Crystal set of methodologies, however, is that it is "human-powered," something also emphasized in the Agile Manifesto.

DSDM

The Dynamic Systems Development Method (DSDM) is an older system that has been adopted within the Agile stable. It uses several techniques to render the product according to loose Agile principles.

- *Facilitated Workshops*
- *Modelling and Iterative Development*
- *MoSCoW Prioritization*
- *Timeboxing*

MoSCoW Prioritization refers to the method of identifying priorities in the project, using the concepts of Must, Should, Could and Won't. Timeboxing is related to the emphasis on establishing the desired quality, expense and time frame of the project at its initiation, in keeping with the Agile approach. This method determines a specific time period (called a time box) to individual planned activities and focuses on meeting smaller, attainable deadline goals.

Like Crystal, the concentration on quality in DSDM requires a member of each team to function as a tester. At the same time, DSDM is designed to be the result of development and input by businesspeople in a business environment, so it regards value as the most important objective of the project. MoSCoW Prioritization allows both the project team and the end-user to determine which requirements of the product are essential and which are optional, so that the end-user does not have unrealistic expectations about what the technology is capable of or what is possible on the available budget of time or money. Time-boxing is merely a method of dividing the project into manageable segments in relation to cost and time.

A possible criticism of DSDM is that it is more administrative than the other sub-approaches. It entails comprehensive studies before work is initiated, and constant customer liaison and feedback once it has begun. Also, the documentation around the project is administered by what is known as a consortium and is not available for free.

M	MUST	*Critical requirement for successful delivery*
S	SHOULD	*High priority, should be included in final product*
C	COULD	*Desireable, included with resources permitting*
W	WONT	*Item will not be included in the final product*

XP (Extreme Programming)

Not to be confused with the Microsoft operating system Windows XP (which is also sometimes referred to simply as XP), Extreme Programming methodology, or XP, is the project of Agile co-establisher Kent Beck (see Chapter 2). On the official site, the discipline is described as follows:

> *"Extreme Programming is a discipline of software development based on values of simplicity, communication, feedback, courage, and respect."*

The following "Core Practices" are outlined:

- *Whole Team*
- *Planning Game, Small Releases, Customer Tests*
- *Simple Design, Pair Programming, Test-Driven Development, Design Improvement*
- *Continuous Integration, Collective Code Ownership, Coding Standard*
- *Metaphor, Sustainable Pace*

XP is the most used software development strategy in the U.S. at time of publication. With its extensive and customer-directed planning philosophy, as well as its utilization of "pair programming" (a tactic in which one programmer tests another programmer's work), it has a sound operational and technical basis. The concept of pair programming is expanded by the adoption of the collective code ownership technique, according to which more than one programmer in the team can work on the same code. This technique is further enhanced by the use of uniform code throughout the entire project. Also, it is the customer who establishes quality tests for the development team to implement.

One identified issue with XP is that it may or may not necessitate the presence of the customer or their representative at the premises of the development team, since the latter is required to participate to such a significant extent in the actual project work. However, some customers may appreciate this approach, so for those end-users who are prepared to take a more active role in the development of their product, XP is a suitable alternative.

CHAPTER FIVE

Tools

A tool in this instance is defined as any physical activity, technique or software program that accomplishes some purpose within the applied management methodology. If the methodology represents the strategy that governs the project work, the tools are used in the implementation of that strategy. For example, if the project team needs to determine how many productive hours certain iterations will require, there are tools available to assist them in this estimation. Some tools are used to assess the entire scope of the project, from its outset to its delivery of the final product, while others are far more immediate and narrow to provide smaller, more localized solutions. These tools are either software programs or are software incorporated, as opposed to older or more traditional tools, such as paper filing systems, Gantt charts or other hard copy planning and assessment systems. Unfortunately, some of the older tools simply do not have the features or capacity to accommodate the techniques used in Agile, since those techniques were not in use when Agile was developed.

Physical Filing/Classification Systems

These systems work to a certain extent and in a software environment. It is unlikely that they would appear as an attractive option to many users. Also, they are not easy to transmit to the customer or to remote members of the development team. Software used in assessments or planning typically does not generate physical copies of its output, unless the user dictates otherwise.

Basic Software Applications

These include the traditional style options such as Microsoft Excel or OpenOffice Calculator (or, for Mac users, Numbers). These applications have served their purpose in the past, but modern team management and product development processes have led to the rise of a sub-industry in the development of software that specifically targets the project environment (see Chapter 10). Project participants may experience that programs like these are too limited or misdirected in their functionality, requiring extreme improvisation in their use (which does not always make a favorable impression on the customer), or even making some operations in Agile impossible to execute.

Specialized Agile Software

These are the applications that have been designed and marketed specifically for the users of Agile methodologies. Therefore, they are the most suitable for deployment in the Agile activities. A number of applications have even been developed by some of the founders of the Agile movement, such as Kent Beck's Extreme Programming.

As with any software, there are open source (freeware) and proprietary programs. The list below mentions some of the most easily available products, but it is by no means exhaustive and is not intended to constitute promotional material. Starting with the proprietary or trademark software, the following programs are available on the market at this time:

VersionOne
PivotalTracker
Rally
Scrumwise (for Scrum teams)
Agile Agenda
Agile Bench
Aldon Agile Manager
Agile Soup (Android app)
Agile Zen
Agile Cockpit

This is not a list in any order of priority, and there are more programs available with more to be released past date of publication. Some of the listed options offer free trial periods, so interested parties are advised to experiment with different software to determine what works best for their specific project situation before investing.

Turning to open source, which may be used at no charge indefinitely, the following products are available for download. Once again, this is not an exhaustive list, and users should be aware that some open source software does not come with any sort of guarantee.

Agilefant	*XP Studio*
ClearWorks	*Xplanner+*
Express	*Retrospectiva*
FireScrum	*Scrinch*
Planigle	*PPTS*

CHAPTER SIX

Practical Implications

This chapter examines the practical issues that arise in situations where Agile is used to manage a project. The issues are categorized under three broad headings: costs, staff and market implications. These categories seem to be appropriate, given that Agile focuses on and seeks to optimize these aspects of project management.

Expense Structure

Any project usually involves expense of some kind. Whether it is the cultivation of beans in plastic holders for an elementary school exercise, or the construction of a bridge over a river with a 200-foot span, expenditure has to be monitored, and usually predicted before work begins. Agile serves to reduce or restrict costs in two ways; one of them is very general in its operation, and the other is more an internal function of how the project is managed.

It has already been mentioned that, as opposed to the more traditional and premeditated Waterfall philosophy of "plan first, do next, see if the budget is met," Agile first establishes the budget and then tries to contain the scope of the project within it. This point of departure is the more general of the two ways in which Agile limits the expense associated with a project. The customer or other project commissioner is assured of two things – first, that they won't have to spend more than they are prepared to, and second, that even if their available resources cannot support the ultimate desired outcome, they will at least be left with something constructive to apply in their organization. This also implies that the customer is never going to be presented with a final result that is not satisfactory to some extent. This eventuality has already been outlined in a preceding chapter. There are some horrific examples of this happening in mega-industry, instances where the development team may have subscribed entirely to the project brief and even overrun the budget and time-frame, but delivered a product that was useless to its end-user or a failure in its target market.

The second and more microcosmic manner in which Agile cuts costs is through its use of quality monitoring and assessment. This happens on a constant basis, especially in methodologies such as XP or Crystal. Contrast this to Lean, which involves the reduction of the unnecessary consumption of resources and associated wastes. A situation in which the end-user is actively present in the project development phase is unlikely to result in excessive costs, since the sponsor will easily become aware of such costs and will then use their discretion to approve or reject execution.

Building a house takes place according to a pre-approved blueprint. But it is perhaps more sensible to have the homeowners present to show them the various stages of construction, so that they can refine or tweak the plans as they desire. In fact, people who commission the construction of their own homes usually take a very intense interest in the process and even resort to their own procurement of materials or specialist artisans if they believe that they are able to do the job more cheaply than the primary contractor. This, then, is one of the strengths of Agile.

Staff Issues

The Scrum style of holding meetings may seem immature or showy. However, it does advertise an attitude of urgency to observers, such as customers. Team members are encouraged to adopt the sentiment that the customer's deadline is important and that they need to approach their tasks with a sense of urgency. This is in contrast to premeditated Waterfall projects that sometimes extend beyond their initial deadline and where, in the final analysis, some operatives are exposed as requiring an inordinate amount of time to complete relatively simple activities. This destroys customer satisfaction and perception, since some of those operatives may have been paid according to the period that they spent working on the project.

To refer back to the immigrants' home construction site once more, imagine the laborers arriving at the site in the morning. They first sit around for about an hour to 90 minutes, drinking coffee and chatting about personal affairs. Then they sluggishly start to chop into the hard ground to excavate the foundation, still conversing about their marriages, finances and sports teams. When the site foreman yells at them to show some enthusiasm, they reply that they still have plenty of time to finish the job. Now compare that scenario with a Sprint meeting. It is obvious which approach business people, and society generally, would rather see in action where their money, market share or other interests are at stake.

Sometimes, project or business management systems necessitate the introduction of a supervisory or facilitator role, which is not an inherent part of the organization itself. This role is either partially or entirely dedicated to the implementation of the system. Its job title may even reflect that capacity. As an example, in Scrum there is the Scrum Master, who does not participate in the concrete project labor but is not entirely a team manager either. There are certain issues related to this phenomenon of dedicated, supplementary roles, whether full or part time, that need to be discussed.

First, the person who occupies the role needs to have an above-average understanding of the system. They need to be trained in its application and procedures. Once implemented, they may also not be available to perform their usual duties. This may become the focus of attrition or antagonism from other staff, since "so-and-so is never at their desk these days" or, as some may ask, "how come they get to go to all the seminars and stuff?"

This type of hostility to implementation needs to be alleviated as soon as possible. Other staff members need to realize that the system is being used for a specific purpose. In introducing the plan to them, the concrete, anticipated ROI or advantages for customer service should be explained in detail, in terms that they can understand. The selection process for the facilitator should also be as transparent as possible, possibly on a voluntary basis. It should be obvious to everyone why a certain person is being used in that role, the extent of his or her new expertise, and why that role is necessary.

Sometimes, employers institute rewards or incentives for staff. This is harder to accomplish where the output of a collective task depends on the contribution of an entire team. Measuring the performance of individual members is not only complicated at times, but also potentially sensitive, especially where the team is engaged in an abnormal or interim endeavor. This is a factor to take into account in selecting and instituting the appropriate Agile methodology.

There is also the usual resistance to new methods, especially where new or atypical techniques are involved. Standing during meetings and using odd terminology are sometimes too hard to accommodate for the less flexible (or more dedicated) members of staff. Once again, the benefits of the system's implementation need to be emphasized at all times.

Another reason why staff need to be properly informed about implementation is that the understanding of importance empowers them to manage the process themselves, either partially or entirely. The Agile system advocates the use of staff under what is largely their own supervision. The prime example of this sentiment is seen in the Scrum methodology, in which no outside person has authority over how the

Development Team manages and executes the actual project labor. The Team manages itself, mostly, and the Scrum Master merely provides relevant information and updates on the progress of the project.

Where staff take ownership of a situation or project, they are easier to motivate, sometimes requiring no prompting at all. Their level of dedication to the success of the initiative is much higher, and they are likely to be more creative in their input, since they are not blindly following instructions or performing to a bare minimum standard set by someone else. An increased sense of responsibility translates into greater attention to quality and more respect for deadlines, which is harder to achieve in the traditional Waterfall paradigm, where the project manager has greater or even absolute authority and the project scope has already been fixed at its outset.

A possible problem attached to the principle of the exceptionally empowered team is that its internal dynamics may sometimes obstruct its progress. Because of its cross-functional nature, some members may have overlapping or identical skill sets, but subscribe to different approaches within the same discipline. This is an obvious territory for dispute and/or paralyzed communication. Another possible objection is that some of the methodologies, XP in particular, might rely on pair programming (see Chapter 4). Not everyone in the software industry supports this technique. However, given the success of XP generally, this seems to be a relatively less significant source of concern.

Market Implications

According to Highsmith, this is one of the focus areas of the Agile movement. The emphasis of Agile is on the development and introduction of new products, so the market is better served by a faster turnaround time on such introduction, either in response to its stated needs or as an improvement upon existing options. Enterprises sometimes also have to react in a short space of time to the sudden release strategy of a competitor.

Agile allows for speedy development procedures. Since the process of development and refinement is executed in stages or iterations, the customer can progressively perfect the product or limit its scope, thus enabling a more immediate introduction to the target market. At the same time, they can release an undeveloped version of the product, but market it as a new advance in the industry, then add the remaining stages to later editions. The constant involvement of the customer in the development process results in greater satisfaction on their part. If they are able to observe the project's progress as it happens, and if they are provided with regular and spontaneous feedback, they may experience the service provided by the developer as superior. Adherence to differentiated time frames is always appreciated, as is staying within the approved budget.

CHAPTER SEVEN

Brief Agile Case Studies

Case Study #1 : GE

Our first case of GE (formerly known as General Electric), shows how the system can be deployed in an industry that is not exclusively centered on the development of software, i.e. that is outside of the pure IT industry. Of course, large corporations usually have an IT department and require development of their own proprietary software, so that is where Agile is most likely to be used.

One example of how GE has used Agile is in its finance department. There, a new software infrastructure was required for crunching numbers so that operatives would be better able to reach informed decisions. Essentially a business analysis intervention, the new software was required to gather data from the existing platforms and make it accessible to the new program. Using traditional methods, the estimated turnaround time on the integration process was between 18 and 24 months.

The integration via the new software, which was executed by GE's own in-house IT department using Agile, took all of one year, inclusive of its implementation. This type of integration is not uncommon in large companies. Some of them maintain enormous databases of customer information and transaction records. Shifting the entire archive of data to a new, more efficient system, or one which has expanded capabilities, may either be a matter of reducing expenses or of necessity due to a changing market environment. The sooner companies are able to conclude the integration, the sooner they can meet the new expectations of their customers or start saving on costs.

By cutting a year off the development time of the software, GE pre-empted not only an additional year of use of their prior systems, but also eliminated 12 months of developmental expense. This was made possible by the Agile methodology. The more traditional approach, of a fixed project scope and an estimated time-frame (such as 18 to 24 months) and budget, would have resulted in at least another 6 months spent in developing the new software.

There also would have been no guarantee as to its absolute suitability. Agile delivers satisfactory pieces one at a time, resulting in an end product that is stable and functional.

Using a more conventional methodology, the summary release of the entire new software package would have necessitated a more sudden and comprehensive integration process, which is not only institutionally traumatic but also causes upheaval among staff who have to be taught en masse in its use on an immediate, accelerated basis. They also have to waste productive time while the IT personnel work overtime transferring all the data to the new platform and trying to understand errors and how to resolve them. Some of these errors may be systemic and could have been avoided through an incremental approach.

The example cited in this chapter isn't the only area of the enterprise where GE has used Agile. The company has also instituted the methodology in its Industrial Internet range of software products for energy producers, the GE Oil & Gas Engineering initiative, which has been publicly reported to make use of Agile software development.

Case Study #2 : Homeland Security

The U.S. Department of Homeland Security ("Homeland Security" or "Department") is an example of a government organization that has implemented Agile in its software development activities. As the federal authority on internal security and border integrity, Homeland Security processes matters such as immigration and the identification of citizens. It has a massive user base (the entire population of the United States), and the standard of its data needs to be impeccable. At the same time, the system used to process and store that data is required to be entirely secure at all times.

The quality of the data and the security of its archiving depend on the sophistication and reliability of the software used by the Department. It is understandable that Homeland Security develops its own software, using its own IT resources, since national databases are highly sensitive and should not be entrusted in their entirety to outside contractors to maintain (even though outsourcing is an existing strategy). In 2013, the Department started to use Agile in its software development (in addition to cloud computing), in an attempt to improve the turnaround time on new projects.

Project Delivery

Homeland Security has an annual budget of approximately $6 billion, with approximately 15% of this budget spent on IT. Agile was implemented in response to an identified weakness in the budgeted delivery of new software products. In 2013, about one in three IT projects exceeded either their budget or delivery time frame. This concern was addressed by instituting Agile techniques. The emphasis of the implementation has been on the user. The developers liaise with users, discuss specific instances of user experience, and then allow the users to be involved in the testing of the new software.

In the sense that the end-user participates directly in the development process, this is an important method of empowering members of the public in the expenditure of government resources. The internal or citizen affairs department in any country may be seen as slow, excessively bureaucratic, or culpable in the unnecessary absorption of public funds. Through engaging the public in the creation and implementation of new systems and procedures, the electorate may be more amenable to the sentiment that tax revenue is being spent wisely and that the service they receive is the optimum possible experience.

Government Contracts

The competition for government business is a traditional aspect of capitalist economies, and proposals for government projects are sometimes fiercely contested. Homeland Security is no exception to this type of attention from private business. As far as software development companies are concerned, the Department has established an innovative niche use of the Agile methodology in awarding contracts. Because Agile development takes place in iterations, it is possible to assign each Sprint to a different contractor. Remember that each Sprint delivers a usable phase of the end product. The entire project can then be spanned over a longer or shorter period of time, postponed, or suspended indefinitely, without the contractor being able to oppose any such decision, or even secure permanent tenure in providing the development service.

This has advantages for government in that an unsatisfactory service provider can be abandoned after their first Sprint involvement. Budgetary discipline and the flexible prioritization of new products are also easier to accomplish. These are two of the primary benefits of the Agile methodology, as illustrated by its application in the government sphere.

CHAPTER EIGHT

Extended Agile Case Study : Yahoo! Inc.

Case Study #3 : Yahoo! Inc.

Yahoo! is a multinational firm known for its web portal, Internet search, and related services. With a $32 billion market cap, the company can certainly be called a "large enterprise." What follows is the summary of a case study presented by Yahoo! Agile practitioner, Gabrielle Benefield, which describes the process Yahoo! took when implementing Agile. The proof here is not in the pudding but in the fact that Yahoo! still retains the Agile method of project management despite some of the challenges they faced during the initial implementation stages.

Implementation

In the environment that is the Internet, the only constant is change. Yahoo!, a company that provides products and services to more than 500 million users worldwide, knew the importance of remaining flexible and adaptive when bringing products to the global, web-based market. Benefield joined the company in 2005 to propel their adoption of Agile project management. The goal, starting with Scrum, was to utilize the lightweight framework that Agile methods provide to create "collaborative self-organizing teams" that "effectively deliver products to market." While the following case study outlines many challenges Yahoo! faced, Benefield considers the implementation a success, citing "tremendous successes and valuable lessons learned."

Yahoo! grew tremendously from what was essentially a startup company to a large enterprise. Initially, in 2002 Yahoo! had begun to merge their startup roots with the need for a standard process to deliver better products faster. This initiative was based on a program called the "Product Development Process" (PDP), a Waterfall type program that had been mandated by Yahoo!'s management. What Benefield found was that many of Yahoo!'s teams and divisions either ignored the process entirely or instead managed to retroactively manufacture participation when they had in fact abandoned the program's methods. Those teams that adhered to the administration's mandated approach found the process more a hindrance than an asset. After debating the top down mandate of Agile or the bottom up grassroots method, the enterprise chose to implement the program with the support of the rank and file first. The focuses of dysfunction were the project and team management portions of operations. There were significant shortfalls in the areas of planning, project management, release management and team interaction. While it was not launched simultaneously, Benefield cites a wish to have launched Agile engineering protocols and project management Scrum methods at the same time. This serves as a cautionary tale; even though the approach was not a top down initiative, it could have benefited from a wider scope.

Initially, four teams volunteered to test the new Agile methods as well as share their experiences with the rest of the organization. Their business units were diverse; they ranged from products for customers (email and photo sharing) to internal tools (small business management). Initially the volunteers committed to four directives.

1. *To complete comprehensive Scrum training*
2. *To work with outside Scrum coaches, especially during the period encompassing the first several sprints*
3. *To use the standardized Scrum protocol outlined by Scrum advocate Ken Schwaber*
4. *To complete at least one sprint*

In keeping with the iterative nature of Scrum and Agile, volunteer teams could opt out of the program any time after the first sprint. Feedback after two months was positive; managers saw positive results, and team members liked the system and the experience. This led to a word-of-mouth circulation of the program within the organization, and the praise generated encouraged other teams to express interest in the Agile method.

In lieu of using external coaches, the enterprise shifted to using an internal Scrum coaching team. The purpose of this team was to promote the benefits of the implementation of Scrum within the organization as well as to provide training, coaching, and support for the teams using Scrum. This included ensuring that key events and programs were followed, such as the aforementioned daily stand up meetings, iteration planning, and sprint retrospectives.

One of the functions of the Agile project management system is to identify deficiencies within an organization. As this happened for Yahoo!, who was making the change from a mandated Waterfall system to a grassroots Agile system, Benefield and her team started addressing issues as they arose and making these fixes available for all teams. This meant that in practice, a solution for one team was a solution for all teams. These solutions were Agile-minded, including reductions in bureaucracy as well as methods of resource planning and portfolio management.

Tracking Progress

Benefield and her team knew that the only method of measurement would have to be transparent and honest. Across the organization, teams who had implemented the process were solicited for feedback. Those who participated in a survey on the newly-implemented programs received custom printed t-shirts. This incentive proved effective but may not be a great fit for every organization. It is the responsibility of management to best determine how to incentivize their workforce. The overall response rate was a surprising 71 percent, 14 points higher for Scrum pilot team members, and the responses revealed the huge benefits and the resistances to change. In addition to the circulating promotion of Scrum, these surveys bolstered other teams to get on board with the Agile method.

Support from Management

Feedback from peers was determined to be the biggest factor in management's comfort level with Scrum's adoption progress. The members of the company (the original author of this case study included) who were tasked with expanding the scope of Scrum within the organization tended to brief managers on the benefits of the new project, not the particulars of its operation. This was a response to the general manager practice of focusing on results rather than methods. Benefield clearly indicates that this led to issues concerning the ability of management to support teams that were dedicated to the adoption of Scrum. It is important to remember that the transition from a mandated Waterfall program to a lightweight adaptive method is a significant change indeed; the fact that Agile remains largely untested contributes to the resistance that some members of management will exhibit.

Coaching

Once the framework was in place for the volunteer teams, Benefield's team implemented their engagement model, which allowed them to coach several teams effectively. Benefield also states that this model was sensitive to the fact that no two teams would face the same challenges and that no two teams would provide the same solutions. This attempt encompassed the concept that some teams may need rapid change to produce a consistently superior product while identifying that some teams would need persuasion and discussion and others would benefit from rapid change and revolution. This spurred a waiting period for management that was based around the need for Scrum coaches to learn the individual needs of each team they coached. Learning this information allowed coaches to tailor the Scrum architecture to fit the needs of their individual business units.

Coaching also meant not forcing Scrum down employees' throats. Scrum was reserved for those who volunteered to take on the challenges of adopting the new project management program. The initial implementation was organized as follows:

Initial Discussion

- *Meet with people within the enterprise who were interested in Scrum and discuss benefits and challenges*
- *Schedule overviews for key members of the team*
- *Organize training and coaching, including Scrum Master training in conjunction with team training*

Preparation & Training

- *Work with Product Owner to develop product backlog*
- *Conduct two-day Scrum training for the whole team*

Coaching

- *For the first sprint the Agile coach would facilitate the following*
- *First sprint planning meeting*
- *First sprint review*
- *First sprint retrospective*

For the second sprint the Agile coach would be present to mentor the Scrum Master during meetings. During the first stages of this process, the Agile coaches were in frequent contact with the teams to keep their adherence to the process on track. Coaches and facilitators would work with other teams as well to accelerate learning, spot issues early, and pursue improvement. Benefield admits that the first three months were challenging, but the teams that adopted Scrum used it to begin to self-organize and were ready for more advanced training.

Scaling Within the Organization

At the end of 2005 Yahoo! had twenty-five teams who were using the Scrum process consistently. Eighty-four percent of team members said the new system was an improvement over the older methods they had been using. However, an internal obstacle arose; a budgetary cycle change forced the entire company to produce more results with fewer resources. This was a challenge for Benefield and her teams, and the company's response is a good example of what to avoid when implementing Agile.

Other teams within the company had heard about how effective Scrum was, either through internal channels or through other professional channels. With little knowledge of implementation or procedure the individual business units determined that Scrum would be a cure-all for their budgetary woes. Instead of using the professional coaches many team leaders resolved to learn Scrum on their own, which lead to inconsistency and poor interaction between teams. The number of teams implementing Scrum, whether with the support of Agile coaches or without, rose by a factor of 10. Benefield and her coaches couldn't keep up with the training progress of each team and as a result the entire program was at risk. Teams were denied coaching on a basis of availability but moved forward regardless.

Benefield concluded that while Scrum is simple and appears

simple, it could cause quite a bit of change within a team and change the dynamic between team members. Not everyone is receptive to change, a fact we all know well. The role of coaches and standardized training is to help develop teams through the transition period in which peeling off layers of administrative control can highlight areas of poor performance and dysfunction within a team. Teams often blamed the Scrum methodology as the cause of their challenges when in fact their reluctance to adopt new processes was the root cause. Another issue that arose, and this very common in many organizations that are attempting to utilize Agile, is that the team claims they have adopted Scrum, top to bottom, and are making excellent progress. A closer look at the team's methods reveals that what they are calling Agile is in fact a series of mini-Waterfalls. This, too, reflects the unwillingness of many people to discard old habits. These challenges can be overcome with focused training and the use of Agile coaches.

Scaling the Budget

Experience showed again and again that the teams that saw focused and dedicated training also saw the most success. In this period, the coaching teams still could not adequately train the growing number of teams that were requesting assistance in their adoption of Scrum. While the implementation program was receiving funding from an internal professional development organization, the demand for training was too great for the number of coaches the program could afford. To make her case for additional funding, Benefield implemented a program to gather metrics concerning the effectiveness of the teams that had received coaching and compare those to the teams that had not.

The first step in this process was to initiate internal case studies and surveys. The surveys found that there were significant differences in satisfaction and performance between the teams that had coaching and those that had not. Unsurprisingly, the teams with a solid Scrum foundation benefited from the coaching and thrived while teams that had a poor foundational base or little to no coaching had many ongoing challenges and difficulties. While top-level management was interested in this data, they needed more evidence to release the funds to increase the number of coaches.

Once an effective measurement system was devised, Benefield's surveys found millions of dollars in savings and massive increases in productivity ranging from 0 percent to nearly 200. The average productivity increase was about 34 percent. Management was thrilled. Interestingly enough, that number has stayed fairly consistent over time as the program has matured. In 2007 (a year later) the average recorded increase in productivity was 39 percent. From this process Benefield learned some key elements about the use of Scrum coaches within Yahoo!. Remember, this data is specific to Yahoo! and may not be applicable to other implementation scenarios.

- *One Agile coach can coach about ten teams per year.*
- *Each team averages ten people (making the ratio of coaches to staff members 1:100).*
- *Based on surveyed results, average productivity improvements were about 30 percent.*

Refining the Process

Once the money materialized, more coaches could be implemented and the program could be scaled effectively. The expanded coaching program also allowed some mistakes that had surfaced to be corrected along the way. Benefield's team has continued to promote Agile within Yahoo! by creating a culture around it. This promotion machine uses t-shirts to mailings that leverage the success stories generated by other teams within the company to promote adoption rates throughout the enterprise. This is a wise method of adoption: bottom up instead of top down.

What We Can Learn

Organizations contemplating the implementation of Agile can learn quite a bit from this case study. It is an exercise in what to do as much as what to avoid. Most important to the entire process is that Yahoo!'s implementation was done from the bottom up with the support and acceptance of the employees, not from the top down as a mandate from the higher level management. The latter scenario is self-defeating in the sense that the creation of an environment in which team members can feel empowered clashes with a managerial assertion of control.

A pitfall, however, was the slow expansion of the coaching team. Organizations need to understand that sweeping changes cannot be effective unless there really is change. Coaches represent a structured and guided path to facilitating that change, and ignoring their role in the process created more work and expense later. This was out of the hands of Benefield's team, but a thorough understanding by all relevant members of the organization would help implement the process.

Gabrielle Banefield's team at Yahoo! worked to adopt Scrum across a large organization by fitting the organization to the program. The following case study summary demonstrates the Intel Corporation's Agile implementation process and how they stretched Scrum to fit their organization's particular needs and protocols.

CHAPTER NINE

Extended Agile Case Study : Intel Corporation

Case Study #4 : Intel Corporation

With annual revenues of $38.3B and employing 86,300 at the time of study, Intel Corp. is a world leader in the production of microprocessors, motherboard chipsets, and flash memory products. The case study's focus is on the Oregon and Pacific (OAP) Product Development Engineering (PDE) team and their implementation of Agile project management methods. The team needed to implement these new methodologies across multiple teams, sites, cultures, and environments. OAP's work product was a test program designed to run automatic testing equipment (ATE). This is uniquely challenging because no off-the-shelf programming could be used; the program uses a proprietary operating system and interface languages.

Prior to the Agile adoption process the team suffered from a number of issues including high turnover rates, poor morale, missed schedules and insane work weeks. These factors alone present challenges, but additionally challenging to the agile mindset was the strong Waterfall culture that existed at Intel as well. Intel decided to implement Scrum at the beginning of a project because during the lower-stress initial stages of the project a strong foundation could be developed, and the best practices created here could be transferred to later stages in the development process.

Preparation & Initialization

The first transition group included six teams with numerous subteams. Intel reached out to Danube Technologies Inc. as a Scrum implementation vendor and began the process of transitioning to the Agile mindset. Initially, twenty or so group and technical leads attended focused training in a two-day workshop. Team leaders agreed to commit to a three-month pilot period during which they would use their training "as is" instead of attempting to fit it to the organization. This is an interesting method to promote adoption, and as the author of the case study, Pat Elwer, notes: "even though the agreement was there, I could already sense a split in the organization into 'pigs' and 'chickens' in terms of supporting Scrum." Working with Scrum consultants Elwer determined some key elements about the Scrum Master position so as not to create conflict or untoward feelings about the role.

- *The Scrum Master role was valued in performance evaluation as having the same weight as "real engineering work rather than administrative overhead."*
- *Team members who became Scrum Master did not have a technical stake in the team's duties.*

These stipulations are unique to Intel's circumstance but helped smooth the process by eliminating conflicts of interest and promoting the value of the new Scrum system. At the end of the three-month process the number of teams to be managed grew from six to seven with an eighth volunteering to implement Scrum. The challenge then became scaling the program across the organization. Using a scaling model that Danube provided, along with best practices learned in the pilot period and input from teams, the program encompassed 12 teams.

Again, with input from Danube, the teams developed methods for managing and fostering dependencies between multiple teams as well as inter-team communication.

What the team learned from this process can be summarized as follows:

- *Adoption is more important than strict adherence.*
- *Volunteerism is a key to successful adoption.*
- *Self-organization is a key to and a result of successful adoption.*

In the spirit of promoting adoption over adherence, deviations from the "by the book" Scrum methods were discussed but not given negative weight. This method also promoted "outside the box" style thinking and accelerated the learning curve for all teams as well as what Ewer refers to as "unity, not uniformity." Visibility also became a critical component in the implementation process, and channels were developed to allow teams to discuss what worked as well as what had proved to be a dead end method. To fit Scrum into the Intel culture and environment the process was adjusted, and what follows is a brief summary of the roles that key team members played in the process and the program.

By the end of the first year, Scrum was fully rooted in the company's decision-making process and was a framework for planning and resource management. Remember, however, that the development is still in the initial "stress-free" stages. The software is only interacting in models. The next step is testing Agile in the execution phase of the process in which the stakes are higher and stress on staff as well as processes is much higher.

Business Owners	• *Senior managers or engineers with oversight of multiple teams & technical issues for all items.* • *Set milestones & worked to determine what features were important at each juncture.*
Product Owners	• *Functional group managers.*
Technical Owners	• *Technical leads who could collaborate to ensure congruence between teams with dependent outputs.* • *Held meetings to turn epics or novels into sprint ready stories.*
Scrum Masters	• *Cross team engineer with no technical stake in the project team he/she was scrum mastering (this prevented a conflict of interest affecting the final product.)*
Teams	• *Team tasked with one particular output of the test suite.* • *Rarely cross-functional.*
Transient	• *Team member with highly specialized skills needed by multiple teams.* • *Moved from team to team as needed by sprints.*
Conduit	• *Team member who represents more than one person. (i.e. contractor, supervisors, or members of a remote team)* • *Can sign up for more story points of work than a normal team member.*
Story Owners	• *A technical expert with perticular knowledge of how to complete a story, who can develop tasks & request participation of certain team members for completion of those tasks.*

The Next Step

When the rubber met the road, so to speak, Elwer cites many surprises. This period in the production phase is when the silicon devices arrive and information must be gathered about the specific path the project will take toward the future. This is a difficult time in for a PDE. In this period one Scrum team abandoned the new process entirely and reverted to W techniques for project management. Some other Scrums disbanded, deciding that they were finished attempting to use the new system. The remaining teams clung to Scrum vigorously if not very effectively. Those teams had been using two-week sprints but found them impossible and shifted to one-day sprints instead. There were daily meetings that planned the next day and reflected on the previous. In this way they collapsed Scrum's prescribed four meetings into a single meeting under the pressure of the production stage.

These meetings demonstrated the core values of Scrum, according to Elwer. Here could be observed business value prioritization, team sizing, adhering to the backlog, peer updates, implementing process improvements and reviewing the work product. These practices gained pace as the team uncovered more and more information about the devices with which they needed to implement their software. The teams that didn't give up on Scrum remained intact and moved through the process, eventually expanding the sprints back to the two-week standard.

Preparing for Manufacturing

As the testing yielded a more and more bug-free program, manufacturing loomed on the horizon. However, Elwer was still struggling with "handoffs" of information. These handoffs are defined as the separation of execution and feedback across multiple people or teams. Also at this time, in response to existing issues in the software, a number of Task Forces were being developed. At Intel, a Task Force is a group of experts who are called to drop everything and address specific issues within development. These are effective combatants against crisis level developmental issues, and their potency was not lost on Elwer. The biggest issue was how to incorporate the Task Force style approach without changing the overall organizational structure. At this stage, the teams that retained Scrum through the developmental process were too involved in the work to restructure effectively. The answer was Scrum Feature teams. Adopting the Task Force style group of technical experts, these teams worked like a Task Force but maintained slots in other teams to give members a cross functionality as well as a "home" within the project. They serve on Feature Teams "on loan" from their home Scrum team and represent high levels of collective expertise. The program was a success, not only with the members of the existing teams but also with management.

Elwer makes a list of what went well and what didn't throughout the Intel adoption of Scrum.

What Went Right

1. The unique nature of the "starting from scratch" coding meant that there was little room for error. Tests were often done on live silicon units instead of in software models. This meant that a strong focus was developed on writing good stories and writing good acceptance criteria. Good stories mean good backlogs and good backlogs mean that the sprints provide their intended results.
    a. *A "pair review" process was developed that called for a developer and product owner to both agree that acceptance criteria have been met.*

2. During the determination of velocity for the next sprint, no

credit was given for stories that were not completed. This "no partial credit" policy forced teams to focus on 100 percent completion. Stories that did not add up to a 100 percent failed for that sprint and dependent tasks couldn't be started.

3. Use of a 9-day sprint model helped create regularity for the teams. This meant that after sprinting for nine days, review, retrospective, and planning meetings were held every other Friday. Teams would be outside of a sprint every other weekend that ultimately improved quality of life and morale. For weekends that fell inside sprints the teams (using their self-organizing capabilities) could decide whether work through the weekend was necessary to complete tasks on time.

4. Using a structured cadence allowed product owners and business owners to change directions if necessary at relatively frequent intervals.
    a. *Collected data showed a 10 to 20 percent loss of velocity if a sprint was interrupted, so a structured cadence allowed the teams to prevent incurring what they called "sprint interrupt tax."*

5. To facilitate the generation of useful metrics like the burndown chart, Intel utilized a central, open access tool that smoothed the transition and allowed for continuous and impediment-free planning. In the instance of Intel, existing programs didn't fit the needs of the organization, so they designed their own. Elwer admits that the current offerings are more developed than they had been, meaning that the need for an organization to produce their own software is significantly less.

6. The term "story point" was developed to refer to projects with complex time requirements and tasks that couldn't easily be described as having duration in "days." This made conveying results to upper management and outsiders much easier.
    a. *Reducing tasks to less than a day was liberating for teams and enlightening for management. Tasks were assigned a degree of difficulty measured in story points. If a task took longer than a day, management could identify that the task was probably suffering from an impediment.*

7. The Daily Scrum meeting was significantly benefited with visuals and graphic representations of progress, with emphasis on the visual burndown chart.

8. Use of incremental review, or review processes that didn't wait until the review meeting, allowed developers to change course if necessary before the end of a sprint.

9. Visibility of the backlog and reliable metrics about performance helped managers adjust expectations and revise plans as necessary.

10. Extensive support from upper level management made the transition a success. Elwer claims that an absence of support would have killed the project.

11. To effectively change the behavior of the team members who were adopting the Scrum methodology, the new behaviors would have to be practiced. Consistent use of the program and sharing of its results has further cemented the Scrum framework into the Intel culture

What Could Have Gone Better

1. In an effort to improve communications across teams and between product owners and their teams, PO's were allowed to serve on their teams. This worked for some, but some teams found themselves being micromanaged. This is the antithesis of self-organization and presented the organization with roadblocks in the areas of communication and lost potential.

2. The maintenance of a large backlog had negative effects on teams. They began to feel as though they were being overwhelmed with requests if anyone at any time could add or edit the backlog.
    a. *A solution Elwer's team developed was to segregate the new backlog request from the existing ones with a high level of transparency. That way the current backlog was minimal but "on queue" tasks could still be accessed and assessed for later sprints.*

Summary of Results

Elwer measures success in four ways: cycle time, performance to schedule, morale, and transparency. Scrum is identified as the source of a 66 percent reduction in cycle time. In regards to performance to schedule, the two-week planning cycle has been maintained for more than a year from date of study release. Missed commitments and schedule slips are virtually eliminated. Morale is trending upwards with improvements in communication and job satisfaction. The transparency the Scrum method provides has uncovered dysfunction such as bugs, impediments, weak tools, and poor engineering habits.

What is most striking about this case study, however, is how the Scrum process was stretched to fit the Intel culture and how that culture was elastic enough to accept the change. In both this example and the example outlined in the previous chapter, the deciding factor in the success of the programs has been the dedication of one leader within the organization. That leader's vision and vigilance has paved the way for other organizations to consider implementing of Agile and assess the benefits that it may bring.

CHAPTER TEN

Criticism of Agile Project Management

Now that the Agile system has been discussed in some detail, it is possible to explore the criticism it has attracted through the years. Any management theory is susceptible to opposition, either by proponents of existing rival schools of thought or by those who have identified areas of potential trouble in the new approach. Agile is no exception.

Customer Input

One of the primary faults that have been observed in Agile stems from its reliance on the feedback of the end-user or customer. Sometimes, if the commissioner of a project is allowed too great a degree of input or choice in its course and output, the ultimate objective becomes obscured or impossible to achieve on the basis of the preceding work. The aggregation of the work may become so distorted or directionless that it cannot be composed into a satisfactory summary result. This issue may be expressed succinctly in the following adage:

"The customer is always right, assuming that they know what they want."

That the customer is not always sure about their ultimate desired outcome is a reality in the IT industry, as well as in other sectors of commerce where the customer is allowed some level of influence in the decision-making process around the nature of the final product. This is seen in the way that some people or organizations can take an inordinate amount of time to choose from the available range of options, or require "consumer guidance" or "specialist advice," even in the selection of such mundane characteristics as color or size. Entire sub-industries of consultants and "experts" have arisen in response to the indecisive nature of financially able yet equally irresolute consumers.

Agile caters to these consumers to a potentially hazardous extent. Giving them the opportunity to provide feedback on a constant basis may cause extra work for the project team or result in conflicting or even directly contradictory instructions regarding the project's scope. If some people are given the chance to change their minds, they will, not so much as a matter of expedience but simply because they appreciate the sense of authority that the exercise endows. Where a substantial amount of their money is involved, they may even feel obliged to enforce that authority, since they are paying to hold it. The customer needs to understand that the mere fact that they have been asked for input does not necessitate that it should be variable or consistently negative. Some customers are in the habit of being intentionally impossible to please. The way in which the project team accommodates that attitude, is more a matter of professional acumen than technical expertise. As former US President Bill Clinton remarked after the provisionally undecided national election at the end of his second term in office:

"The people of America have spoken, but it's not clear what they said."

This eventuality is one to which Agile is susceptible. It should be addressed through proper communication with the customer at all times, particularly at the outset of the project, where the risk of it arising should be outlined and explicitly discouraged.

Professional Impression/Corporate Image

Effective communication itself requires time and expense to be sustained. Therefore, any management paradigm that relies on constant communication increases this item of the budget, cutting into the profit margin for the development team and representing a possible source of conflict with the customer. Some customers might not appreciate continuous requests for comment or testing, especially if they are not very skilled in the use of IT or they believe that they pay people to solve such problems for them.

How a business communicates with customers and other outside entities is germane to its public image. At the same time, its inner workings contribute to that image too. Customers need to be presented with a professional, suitably constituted philosophy on business and customer service. Some customers may experience the Agile environment as the opposite of that. The fact that the Agile team is often temporary in nature may endow it with a sense of having an improvisatory or maverick status. Also, because it is supposed to be relatively more informal than conventional, it may seem too bohemian or artistic to customers who subscribe to a more staid, traditional approach toward supplier relations and product development.

Lastly, Agile does not emphasize the bureaucracy of the project system. Some operators may see this as a source of relief, but it is potentially a disadvantage. They may not even understand how to use the documentation, or they may regard the compilation of their own training material as an undue expense item in the total project budget.

Team Composition

Staying with the issue of project documentation, more traditional project management systems require production in a comprehensive fashion. Together with a larger staff, this ensures that the absence or departure of a team member does not obstruct the future progress of the project. Agile, on the other hand, is susceptible to this type of impediment, since it uses smaller teams and minimal literature or record keeping.

Dependency of Interrelated Stages

Sometimes, the development of the final product relies on the sequential construction of its component parts, and the later and final phases can only be executed if the preceding ones already have been finished. In project management, this is known as dependency. It is relevant to the metaphor of the immigrants' home, in that the basement can only be built once the foundations have been laid. In subsequent construction work, the ground floor can obviously only be erected if the basement has been completed, and so on.

Agile has been criticized because it does not specifically provide for the planning of interdependency within the project. As such, this seems to be a mostly insubstantial point of concern, since the incremental nature of the system results in a steady supply of finite deliverables that interact and comprise the entire finished item. Their interaction is based on their interdependence, so it is apparent that in scheduling the work, the project team would have to incorporate that aspect as an inherent feature of their project roster.

If Agile does not provide a dedicated tool for that aspect, it is perhaps due to the assumption that the project team consists of highly qualified professionals who are not operating on the basis of the linear, unidirectional Waterfall methodology and thus have an entire understanding of how the project iterations fit together and will automatically realize which elements are dependent on one another. This is possible because the relatively smaller Agile team is responsible for the project in its entirety, as opposed to the more traditional massive project workforces, which are compartmentalized to the extent that some staff may not have any idea where exactly their output is situated in the overarching scheme of the project.

In Agile, there is also the issue of restrictive iterations. Because the iterations are fixed in their duration and output, sudden adjustments to the scope of the project can necessitate additional sprints. These instantaneous modifications are inherent in the Agile methodology and so, instead of stabilizing the budget and turnaround time, the Agile approach could actually serve to expand them. However, as always, that expansion is only going to be translated into a practical outcome if the customer permits it. If the customer decides to stay with their original budget and duration, they may be obliged to accept a product that is less sophisticated or otherwise developed than what they had hoped for or subsequently realized they needed.

Waterfall

This book has already mentioned the project management strategy known as Waterfall, and has provided a rough outline of how it operates, but for the sake of convenience, it will now be summarized again. The Waterfall methodology is regarded as traditional or even "conventional" in that it entails a classic plan-execute-observe approach. The problem or market expectation is identified, a response is planned, and then the project work is performed. Afterwards, such as after the release of a new product, the results of the project can be monitored and analyzed.

The typical phases in a waterfall project are as follows:

Conception
Initiation
Analysis
Design
Construction
Testing
Implementation
Maintenance

There is no need to enter into an examination of all the various methods associated with the different phases of this strategy. Obviously, software plays a part in its execution, but the primary sequence of stages remains unchanged. Some may describe it as adhering to a generic rationale or demonstrating a natural progression, in that it maps out how informal, unplanned projects will run their course anyway.

What has also been noted about the Waterfall methodology is that it generates a rigid project scope, but only an estimated budget and time frame. Therefore, it is prone to cost more or take longer than anticipated. It also does not necessarily deliver a product that is entirely or even remotely adequate to the desired outcome of its introduction or deployment.

WATERFALL	AGILE
Fixed Scope	Variable Scope
Single Execution Phase	Iterations (Sprints)
Summary Delivery	Incremental Delivery
Estimated Budget & Time Frame	Established Budget & Turn Around Time
Inflexible Blueprint	Constant Adjustment of Scope as Possible
Limited Opportunity for Feedback	Iterative Feedback Required
Top-Down Management	Self-Managed Teams
Less Transparent Management	More Transparent Management
Segregation of Skills	Cross-Functional Teams
Extensive Administration	Minimum Bureaucracy
End-User Examines Finished Items	End-User Tests & Makes Increments
Terminates Only on Completion	Possible End-Point After Each Iteration

Considerations such as these are typically raised where Waterfall is compared to Agile. This juxtaposition is an unsurprising exercise in the management advisory industry (see Chapter 11), but it is not merely due to professional rivalry or intellectual one-upmanship. The advantages of Agile over Waterfall have been established in practical applications, not limited to the IT industry. The two case studies in this text serve as proof of that. What may limit the extent of the evidence at this time is the relatively short history of the Agile methodology. It was only officially inaugurated as a project management philosophy at the start of the 21st century, and the literature and operating track record of the system are not as prolific as those of the older approaches. Therefore, it is possible for objections to Agile to rise because it is a "new" system of management. This lack of evidence and make project management practitioners belive that it is unreliable, or at the very least an unknown quantity. Where valuable resources of time and capital are at stake, some economic role-players prefer to stay away from what they see as unproven or precariously novel attitudes. They may also refer to their traditional organizational culture in making this assertion.

However, after more than ten years in service and a publicly reported resume of success in both big business and government, this objection is starting to seem increasingly false and inflexible. As more enterprises adopt the Agile methodology in one form or another, those who remain steadfast in their Waterfall or other approaches may start to lose market share or industry stature. Alternatively, those who do not remain adherent to traditional methods may experience progress in the opposite direction, either through increased customer numbers and retention or by association with other esteemed companies who use Agile. What follows is a short summary in table form of the main differences between Agile and Waterfall. It is probably one of the most published diagrams in project management literature at this time, but no publication on the subject of Agile would be complete without it.

The system that is used depends on the nature of the project and the required staff complement. There is no established purpose in trying to ascertain the superiority of one system over the other. In some instances, one may be more or less suitable than the other. Project managers simply have to try to match a system to their specific project characteristics.

CHAPTER ELEVEN

The Agile Sub-Industry

As is the case with other management systems, such as business or organizational management methodologies, Agile has attracted a sub-industry of experts, practitioners and product suppliers. These professionals rely on their advanced knowledge of the Agile system and its methods to provide advisory and implementation services to their customers. Some of these firms also design and publish Agile tools, such as the software described in Chapter 6. Business and project management are officially recognized fields of activity these days, so the initiation and advocacy of this type of sub-industry is not limited to the Agile paradigm.

The Sub-Industry

Some experts may offer Agile techniques as part of their entire portfolio of management options. Other are dedicated exclusively to Agile. This sole focus is seen among those who established the paradigm, such as Kent Beck, the founding authority on XP (Extreme Programming), who has a site committed to XP and Agile. The extent to which this sub-industry has achieved success or is proliferating is a matter of future observation. In relative terms, Agile is a very new management discipline and, although it has been adopted by thousands of firms, its true longevity will only become apparent after a matter of decades.

There are two possible apparent impediments to its progress. The first is that Agile is not a broad enough discipline to merit official academic status. It cannot stand on its own as a subject. It is merely one of a variety of project management approaches, and it does not independently possess the magnitude or complexity of subject matter to constitute a separate field of study.

At the same time, because it is so lacking in complexity and minimal in its philosophy and methods, it can be assimilated into an organization's processes without outside assistance. Management can easily examine and apply its procedures. The fact that the software tools are openly available on the market, sometimes at no charge, enables the frequency of this occurrence. Contrast this to business management systems such as Six Sigma, which requires advanced statistical expertise to master, or the Toyota Production System (Toyotism), which affects the entire organization top to bottom.

The absence of more official academic recognition deprives a subject of supporting infrastructure. Its promotion and development then relies on the contributions of its loyal proponents, which are more sporadic and undeveloped than the regulated, officially sanctioned and sponsored study and improvement enjoyed by more traditional disciplines. There are, however, organizations with authority in the industry; the foremost of these being the Agile Alliance, a non-profit organization which offers registered membership and aims at an international subscription. The Alliance undertakes academic research projects and endorses workshops and conferences.

Another option, which is focused specifically on Scrum, is SCRUMstudy. SCRUMstudy administers certification programs for those who wish to practice as Scrum experts, either as employees in an enterprise or as management advisers. Trainees are required to pay fees and pass examinations. These courses can be undertaken through the international network of partners with whom SCRUMstudy is associated.

Literature

Literature on Agile might not be as substantial or easy to obtain as that of other management systems. The new nature of the paradigm translates into a shortage of published subject matter. Most of the literature, therefore, is comprised of articles and papers, however; for those who desire to conduct further reading, one important work to consider is the book written by one of the 17 founders. Jim Highsmith is at the top of the list below:

1. *Agile Project Management : Creating Innovative Products* (2nd edition) by Jim Highsmith (2009)
2. *Coaching Agile Teams* by Lyssa Adkins (2010)
3. *Agile Testing : A Practical Guide for Testers and Agile Teams* by Lisa Crispin and Janet Gregory (2009)
4. *Enterprise and Scrum* by Ken Schwaber (2007)
5. *Scrum Shortcuts without Cutting Corners : Agile Tactics, Tools and Tips* by Ilan Goldstein (2013)

Schwaber (item 4) is another of the 17 Agile founders. Besides these works, readers are advised to peruse the periphery material available online.

CONCLUSION

The software industry is a modern phenomenon and, as such, the techniques of management and product development that it entails are somewhat unique to its character and product. To say that Agile could only have originated from this industry is not entirely accurate, but it is a partially cogent statement nonetheless. Perhaps Agile merely required the environment presented by the IT sector to be more formally adopted. As a member of the more general catalog of project and business management techniques, Agile has a worthy position and offers an effective approach to the management of suitable projects. Its efficacy has been proven by its diverse, extensive application in practice and its stature in discussions of management systems.

The extent to which it progresses into the future, in terms of both its expansion and refinement, remains to be seen. However, the simplicity and universal relevance of its principles and innate philosophy would appear to suggest that it will be present in management textbooks for some time. Agile may start to acquire an even greater presence as more and more industrial activity relies on IT and the development of custom software.

One should also remember that some principles in management are timeless. Just as those 20th century immigrants slowly but patiently constructed their homes piece by piece in their new country, so too does Agile represent some of the overriding concepts in business, management and the design and release of new products in any industry. Perhaps instead, Agile is more representative of the culmination of a long-term evolution, supported now by technology that more entirely enables its effective implementation, than a trendy catchphrase or a temporary phase. As far as its success is concerned: only time will tell.

We at ClydeBank Media would really like to thank you for purchasing our book. As a token of our appreciation, please take advantage of the Free Gift that was presented in the beginning of this book – access to the Agile & Scrum learning community.

AGILE PROJECT MANAGEMENT MASTERY

AN ADVANCED GUIDE TO AGILE PROJECT MANAGEMENT

CONTENTS

How To Use This Book

This book is an in-depth look at the Agile Project Management system. Chapter 1 presents a brief overview and definition of project management, and an examination of the principles of project management follows in Chapter 2. Chapter 3 furthers the study of project management by reviewing the different phases that occur throughout the life of a project.

The emphasis on Agile commences in Chapter 4 with an examination of its principles. In Chapter 5, the relationship between Agile and Lean is discussed, and Chapter 6 discusses the relationship between Agile and Six Sigma. Some of the more common methodologies of Agile software development are examined in Chapter 7 while Chapters 8, 9 and 10 offer a more in-depth review of Agile project management.
A list of additional resources is presented following the conclusion.

Those interested in applying Agile to their projects, however they intend to use it, should remember that the information provided here is general in nature and does not constitute specific professional advice or organizational strategy. However, as a preliminary source of information, it will enable the reader to pursue deeper inquiries and ultimately decide on the suitability of the system and, once that has been established, the exact variation to apply.

INTRODUCTION

Project management has its roots in government and military projects that were undertaken on large, and sometimes massive scales. In the study of project management, it is important to differentiate between the terms "program" (program management) and "project" (project management). A program typically consists of a number of separately managed but interconnected projects that have a common objective. Imagine the Egyptians conceiving the Great Pyramids and all of the individual projects that were undertaken in support of the program goals. It is estimated that the construction of the pyramids took several hundred to over a thousand years to complete. This could either be thought of as the largest and longest-running program in the history of the world or the as a number of consecutive projects, each merely mimicking the goal of the previous ones. Even so, some of the pyramids took over 20 years to construct. Not even one of the most massive projects of the modern day, the Three Gorges Dam in China took that long to construct, though it was so massive that when completed, the redistribution of water mass had an effect on the rotation of the Earth itself. The Agile approach to project management was not originally conceived or developed as a system of project management per se, but rather as a sustainable system of managing ongoing software development projects - a kind of program management system. Incidentally, Agile is not really a system at all. It is a set of principles that can be applied to project management best practices. Like the building of the pyramids, Agile focuses on sustainability - long-term growth without depletion of resources.

This book will examine specific strategies for implementing Agile principles of software development into the practice of project management. Agile was conceived by developers in response to the traditional methods of developing software in a rapidly-changing environment of user-driven requirements. In the mid-1990s, computer software was being developed at an unprecedented rate, and it was not uncommon for bugs and inadequacies to be discovered in a program only after it had been released to customers. Pioneering developers recognized the rapidly changing pace and requirements of the software development field and devised a system of managing software projects that they called Agile. This book will blend Agile, Lean and Six Sigma philosophies to present specific strategies for managing projects in any field, be it software development or constructing a building.

There is quite a bit of overlap between the principles of Agile software development and the strategies that are utilized in Lean to reduce waste and increase profit, as well as between Agile principles and Six Sigma. Lean focuses on reducing waste and maximizing efficiency. Six Sigma is focused on the reduction and control of errors, and it is obviously a seamless match for a blending with Lean. Both Lean and Six Sigma were developed as organization-wide philosophies, while Agile was developed to be project-specific. Agile can be utilized to effectively manage virtually any project with very little or no modification to its principles. The discussion of integrating Agile with both Lean and Six Sigma principles and strategies that follows is included with the assumption that the reader has sufficient grasp on the concepts and practices of Lean and Six Sigma.

As with the Lean and Six Sigma movements, Agile has become popular in the sub-industry of professional consulting and project management software and tools. Unlike a number of project management philosophies, Agile does not actually require a unique project in order to be effective. This book will examine the practice of engaging consultants and tools to assist with applying Agile principles to both everyday unique projects and organization-wide operations.

CHAPTER ONE

Defining Project Management

The Project Management Institute (PMI) is a leading not-for-profit professional organization for the project management profession, and it states that a project must be *temporary*, with a defined beginning and end. Consequently, the PMI definition also requires that a project have a defined scope and defined resources. The scope of a project must be specific in detail with a defined goal. The resources that are to contribute to the completion of a project must be defined and quantified. Note the focus on the fact that these characteristics must be defined. A project must also be unique. It is not merely a routine or repeating operation or task; it is a set of tasks that are arranged and intended to accomplish a singular outcome. While the building of a bridge may seem like a project, without further definition it is not. If the goal is a completed bridge, there must be a timeline (when to start building the bridge and when to have it completed) and a defined scope (the location, size and type of bridge to be built and any other relevant specifications), in order for it to be considered a project. Without resources, there is no one to build the bridge and nothing with which to build it.

PMI specifically defines project management as: "the application of knowledge, skills and techniques to execute projects effectively and efficiently." One must be able to define and qualify a project in order to practice project management. PMI further adds that project management is "a strategic competency for organizations, enabling them to tie project results to business goals..." The business goals are the timely completions of projects without using more resources than were originally allocated to the projects. In the profession of project management, these are two important metrics that are termed *on-time and on-budget*. Another critical metric is the ultimate satisfaction of the customer. An on-time and on-budget project does not automatically result in a satisfied customer. In fact, the customer may not even care about either of these metrics. Further complicating matters, the customer may not care whether or not the completed project meets the specifications they provided in the first place. One of the fundamental principles behind the Agile methodology indicates that the customer's expectations throughout the life of a project can change, thus changing the desired end result of the project. It is Agile project's ability to react to changing expectations that makes it truly successful. There is nothing wrong with adding the requirement that a completed project must meet specifications in order to be successful, as long as the project team fully understands that the specifications can, do, and most likely will change throughout the life of the project.

With a definition of both a project and *project management* now on the table, *the principles of project management* can be more easily discussed. There is no single consensus amongst the different project management methodologies as to what the principles of project management are. Some methodologies do agree on certain principal ideas, and most methodologies would not disagree with any one methodology's principal ideas. The following chapter will examine both the definition of a principle, and the principles of project management.

CHAPTER TWO

Core Principles of Project Management

In this chapter some of the basic principles of project management are briefly examined in order to provide a reference point for the following chapters. The most important principles of project management are:

Scope : There must be an actual project with a defined scope or goal. A project is not a regular, ongoing activity. Rather, it has a unique end result for an end user or customer. The scope, or the specifications that define the end result of a project, must be identified before any project task can be started.

Project Manager : In most cases, a single leader is appointed to manage the project. There are, however, instances when multiple project managers involved with the execution of one single project. Project managers should be experienced and committed to managing the project, and must accept responsibility for every task that is to be completed throughout the project duration.

Support : The project manager must have adequate authority to utilize resources and assign tasks to team members as needed. This requires an informed sponsor or management that is willing to give the project manager the authority that he or she needs.

Planning : Project management requires an appropriate plan for the completion of the project. At a minimum, the project plan addresses the "5 Ws" of a project: What the project (or problem) is, Why the project is necessary, Where it is to occur (the question of "where" may refer to more than a physical location, but where within an organization), When the project needs to be completed, and Who (or which resources) will work on it. A project plan includes the various activities and tasks that need to be completed in order for the project to be successful. The project plan should be represented "on paper" (or on screen) with an identifiable critical path signifying the sequence of events that must be achieved in order for the project to be completed. Each task in the plan, the specific resources allocated to it, and the estimated cost of those resources and the time that is expected to complete the task are included in the plan.

Schedule : Project management requires that there be a defined start and an end date. A schedule is more than a set of dates, or the answer to the "when" in the 5 Ws. More precisely, it is a visual representation of tasks and activities and their start and dates, and it should represent the interdependence between those tasks. Milestones (significant indications of progress) and deliverables should be easily identifiable in a project schedule. A perfect project plan should function as a schedule.

Resources : A project must have finite resources that are allocated to it. These resources include a dedicated team of appropriately experienced personnel, an appropriate budget and any other resources that are required for the completion of the project.

Change : Project management requires the welcome accommodation of change. Change in this context should not be confused with scope creep, or the tendency for the scope of a project to grow unchecked. Accommodating change is a fundamental principle of customer satisfaction. Project management includes planned reactions to change, reactions that have been tested and shown to be effective in managing change. The aforementioned seven principles are the essence of project management. While some methodologies provide for additional principles, none would disagree with any of these. The application of knowledge, skills and techniques to execute projects effectively and efficiently can be best accomplished by adhering to guidelines that are based on these principles.

In Chapter 4, the principles of project management will further examined down to their fundamental qualities, and the principles of Agile will be examined in context.

CHAPTER THREE

Project Phases

In addition to recognizing and utilizing basic principles of project management, it is important to recognize the typical stages of a project. As a project progresses from its inception through its planning, execution and completion, there are specific phases, or steps that the process of managing a project undergoes. Various project management methodologies identify these steps. Although some differ from one methodology to the next, the underlying theme is consistent. According to PMI's Project Management Book Of Knowledge (PMBOK), there are five such phases, which the PMBOK identifies as process groups. These process groups identify the phases of the life cycle of a project.

Project Phases From PMBOK

Initiation : The initiation of a project takes place when the project is conceived. An end-goal is identified, and the scope is defined with specifications that help define the goal. Typically, only the sponsors of a project are involved in this phase, though they may choose a project manager and introduce him or her to the project during this phase.

Planning : During the planning phase, the scope of a project is refined and the boundaries of the scope are identified. The processes that are required to achieve the desired results of the project are identified and sequenced in order to develop a project plan. Processes are designed to produce results that meet the specifications that were identified in the initiation phase, and in some cases, additional specifications are identified. Some methodologies combine the initiation and the planning phases into a single phase. The project manager should be involved in this phase, as should the sponsors of the project.

Execution : During the execution phase, the processes that were identified in the planning stage are completed. These processes are completed according to the specifications that were identified in the initiation and planning phases.

Monitoring & Controlling : This phase of the project utilizes metrics to measure the progress of a project. Periodic milestones or deliverables are either met or not, and a plan is in place to react to either case. The progress of a project is measured, and the need for any changes to either the plan or the specifications (or scope) is identified. In some cases this phase leads back to the planning phase. In each case, the monitoring of a specific metric must lead to a specific pre-planned action that is to take place, whether the metric meets, exceeds or fails to meet expectations.

Closing : Some methodologies refer to this phase as the follow-up, follow-through, or even maintenance phase. The activities that take place during this phase are conducted to finalize all other activities and to ensure that the end goal has been accomplished and the customer is satisfied. Various project management methodologies may differ in their listings of the principles of project management, but they will rarely disagree. On the surface the principles and practices may seem different, but under further examination, it is revealed that the basic premise or idea is the same.

Agile Project Phases

The phases, or stages of an Agile project are hardly different from those of the PMBOK:

Envision : The Agile methodology uses the envision phase to initially explore the scope of the project and its objectives. Project team members are identified or proposed. In practice, there is no disagreement between Agile's envision phase and PMBOK's initiation phase.

Speculation : Agile's speculate phase is comparable to PMBOK's planning phase. The project team's or organization's capabilities, needs and risks are identified. Collaboration with customers occurs, intelligence is analyzed, data is collected and costs are estimated. The startup activities of a project are planned.

Explore & Adapt : These two phases of Agile projects are comparable to the PMBOK phases of execution, and monitoring and controlling. In either methodology, these two phases can be grouped together as a continuous cycle throughout the life of a project. They involve managing workload and operations, design and redesign, decision-making and collaboration, measuring progress, reporting and evaluating results, and adaptation to foster improvement.

Close : Agile lists the final phase as the activities to close a project, similar to PMBOK. The importance of the closing phase can be easily expressed in a simple example. Consider a large heating, ventilation and air conditioning (HVAC) company that has just installed an HVAC system in a new building. The installation met all of the requirements of a project, and it was managed as a project by an assigned project manager with a dedicated team. The project was large enough to take several months to complete. In an attempt to follow a Lean strategy, the project manager scheduled deliveries of raw materials in Just-In-Time (JIT) fashion, anticipating the number of sheet metal screws that his installers would use each week.

Unfortunately, the project manager failed to use a Kanban system, in which the deliveries of sheet metal screws would only occur when a demand was evident. The project manager was not concerned about overestimating the usage as the HVAC company uses these particular screws often, and the project manager rationalized that any excess screws would be used eventually. However, the project manager did not take all of the steps to close out the project, one step being to contact vendors and let them know that the project was completed, and that no more deliveries of consumables, like screws, would be needed. The HVAC project was delivered on time and under budget, to the satisfaction of the building owner who promptly paid the HVAC contractor for the work. With no closeout, the weekly deliveries of screws continued, and the HVAC contractor's warehouse workers simply kept stocking the deliveries, and the billing for those screws continued until the entire project's profit was consumed by an excessive inventory of sheet metal screws. Closing is one of the most important phases of a project. It includes ensuring that all changes to the project have been addressed and billed, all resources have stopped working on a project, and all project data is documented, evaluated, and reported to management or the appropriate project sponsors. The customer or end user is asked to approve or "sign off" on the project completion, or the end result is evaluated for conformance with specifications. All costs and resources are accounted for and documented. Finally, any rewards or incentives that were used as a motivational tool should be dispersed according to the performance of team members. Failing to fully close a project can be disastrous to profitability, as well as to the success of future projects.

The phases of an Agile project are easily definable; however, the nature of Agile projects is sometimes contradictory to the notion of following a strict guideline of phases. In particular, the closing phase can be difficult to justify given the continuous nature of Agile software development projects. It is conceivable, and often reality, that a project is ongoing, existing in recurring cycles. One of the more important aspects of the closing phase is the evaluation of the end product and the customer's satisfaction. It is at this point in a project life cycle that the decision must be made whether or not to initiate a new project. A very simple example would be the evaluation of operating system software. An operating system software project is completed, tested, and found to conform to specifications. It is released to the public, which consists of millions of users, making the odds understandably high that a problem or bug in the software will be found. User feedback is evaluated in the closing phase, and it is determined that a new project should commence that will address all of the bugs that the users have reported. Figuratively speaking, the Windows XP project is closed, and the Windows Vista project is initiated. Eventually, the Windows Vista project is closed, and Windows 7 project is initiated. Agile project management is not merely a method, it is a sustainable process based on certain principles. The following chapter will address Agile principles, both fundamentally and as they are applied to the practices of project management.

CHAPTER FOUR

Principles of Agile Project Management

The Agile methodology lists *12 principles* in its Agile Manifesto, some of which specifically focus on software development projects. With only slight modification, the software development-themed principles can be applied to any project, including those that are outside the software development industry. The following briefly explains each of the principles listed on the not-for-profit website, agilemanifesto.org: The Twelve Principles of Agile Software. Even before examining the twelve principles of Agile software development, it is useful to consider the key points that are defined in the Agile Manifesto:

Individuals & interactions are more highly valued than processes and tools. This concept is often considered a departure from Lean and Six Sigma thinking, but upon examination it can be justified to support both schools of thought.

Working Software is valued over comprehensive documentation. Six Sigma's emphasis on measurement and documentation as a means to improve efficiency may seem contradictory, but again, the contradiction is only superficial. Agile prescribes that results are more important than documentation, and they are, but it is also important to know how the results were achieved without expending unnecessary resources.

1. The *first principle* prioritizes customer satisfaction. Whether the customer wants newly developed software or a renovated 20-story building, the first principle focuses on value as defined by the customer. It also emphasizes delivering the software early

and often, software that provides value to the user. Customer satisfaction largely determines the project's success, often regardless of on-time and on-budget completion, and may merely be based on the customer's perception of value. However, the earlier and the more often the deliverables of any project are delivered, the better a project can be monitored and the greater the opportunity for improvement of the overall project.

2. The ***second principle*** makes it clear that changes to the project, even late in the completion process, are welcome. Changes to a project can give a customer a competitive advantage. An apartment building owner whose project team can quickly react to new legislation governing residential building energy efficiency will have an advantage over a competitor who would need to engage a team of engineers to redesign a building from scratch.

3. The ***third principle*** is project turnaround. The faster a project can be completed, the better, not only from the customer's perspective but from the project team's perspective as well. Agile focuses on delivering "working software" projects that may take from mere weeks to months, with a preference for the shorter time period. Outside the software development industry, the reality is that a project may take a few weeks, or it may take several years. Either way, the project team needs to complete a project on time and start the customer's next (or the next customer's) project as soon as possible, without negatively affecting a current or future project. The mention of *working software* in the Agile principles refers to quality, and the preference for faster turnaround is intended to show the importance of both customer satisfaction and efficiency.

4. The *fourth principle* in Agile project management is the role of business resources and senior management in the success of a project. The people who are responsible for the operation of a business or organization must work with the people who are responsible for managing a project, towards the same goal. This cooperation must be ongoing and daily. Without it, the project loses the support of delegated authority and is at risk of failure.

5. The *fifth principle* is based on building projects around motivated personnel. This principle recognizes the possibility that the success of the project is often more dependent on the people involved in completing the project than it is on the goal of the project itself, and that sometimes a project plan should take into consideration the resources that are allocated to the project before defining what the actual project goal is. This concept is obviously at risk of seeming counterintuitive. Just as important are the motivation, working environment, the support and the trust that is given to the people who are working on the project. The order of importance of these factors may not seem significant, but there is a definite connection between each of them. The more trust and support that is given to an individual, the more motivated that individual will be, and vise-versa. The working environment is also a factor in team motivation, and vise-versa.

6. The *sixth principle*, states that the most efficient, productive communication within a project team takes place face-to-face. Like the fifth principle, this can seem counterintuitive, particularly given that a well-written email can be sent in 30 seconds, while a face-to-face meeting can require several minutes at least and hours at most. Agile face-to-face communication is

practiced in a stand-up meeting, which is also well-known in Lean Six Sigma.

7. The *seventh principle* is that "working software" is the primary measure of progress. This concept can be easily modified to apply to a broader range of applications outside of software development. Tracking the success of a project with specific measurements of progress is a best practice, and this also exists in Lean Six Sigma. This principle calls for "working" software, that is, something that fulfills its purpose, and is consistent with the goal of providing value in the first principle.

8. The *eighth principle* states that Agile processes promote sustainable development that leaves room for improvement and growth without depleting the available resources. Sustainable development is not merely an environmentally-friendly buzzword. It is a culture of constant progress. Agile software is never "good enough." Expectations constantly change, and the software must continuously evolve. It isn't difficult to apply this concept to any other project. Building a 30-story residential apartment building, for example, sustainability allows various building components to be easily replaced as continuous advancements, like high performance glass coatings, allow buildings to become more energy efficient.

9. Strongly related to the seventh, the *ninth principle* focuses on what it takes to enhance agility. Like many of the other principles, the ninth requires continuous effort, but it adds a focus on what Agile calls "technical excellence and good design," both of which add value to the end user's product, whether it's a building or a software package. "Good design" is a relatively

simple concept, but "technical excellence" is challenging and requires an attention to detail that goes beyond the mere meeting of specifications.

10. The *tenth principle* is a simple one. It places an emphasis on simplicity itself and is closely related to the waste reduction concepts in Lean. Interestingly, the tenth principle calls simplicity "the art of maximizing the amount of work not done." Lean places value on "value added" work. Any resources that are expended in a process, to perform work that does not add value to the product or service for which the customer is paying, is considered waste and should simply be reduced. By continuously evaluating a project for waste, the opportunity for value and profit will increase.

11. The *eleventh principle* states, "The best architectures, requirements and designs emerge from self organizing teams." On the surface, it may sound specific to software development, until one considers additional uses of the word "architecture," which is really just a specific type of design, and of course requirements can be anything from a specific schedule to specific performance specifications, which can be metrics for any project. Agile places value on self-organizing teams. Each team member naturally gravitates into the most effective role for that respective team member, given his or her natural strengths and abilities.

12. The *twelfth principle*, with its emphasis on communication, can be tied back to the sixth. While the sixth merely focuses on the premise that face-to-face communication is the best form of communication, the twelfth places an emphasis on regularity

> and purpose, stating that a team should regularly review its performance, generate ideas for improvement and then develop and follow through with a plan to make improvements. Stepping outside the realm of software development, this strategy is valuablc to any project, even the regular operations of an organization. The team should meet daily for no longer than 15 minutes. Sometimes the meeting requires more time, though it does not need to be as often as a daily stand-up meeting. It can be accomplished on a weekly basis and should focus on quickly reviewing activities and behavior to identify measurable improvements that can be easily made before the next meeting.

Agile principles are originally intended for software development projects. However, its themes are conducive to best practices in project management as a profession. A professional project manager should be capable of managing any project, regardless of its scope, field or area of expertise. None of the twelve principles of Agile software explicitly state that expertise in software development is required in order to manage a project. Agile project management is more than simply adhering to a set of twelve principles, and the principles of project management are not limited to any single list. While the principles of project management may vary from industry to industry and from methodology to methodology, there are certain *fundamental* principles that can be identified in any successful project management strategy.

A fundamental principle should include the expression of a *basic idea*, or an idea that is a *required* contribution to the success of a project. A fundamental principle should be applicable to any type of project in any industry as a key factor in achieving success, and it should be simple enough to adequately describe the goal in a few sentences. Experienced project managers should recognize a fundamental principle as *self-evident* and should only need a word or two to describe it. A fundamental principle also provides the means to explore practices and to reasonably test them for value. These basic terms apply *fundamental principle* logic to the Agile principles in terms that can be easily adapted to any project:

Customer Satisfaction	*Metrics*
Accommodation to Change	*Sustainable Progress*
On-Time Deliverables	*Attention to Excellence*
Teamwork	*Minimal Waste*
Motivation	*Self-Organization*
Constant Communication	*Continuous Improvement*

With this in mind, an experienced project manager with expertise in building a house should be able to apply his or her expertise to successfully complete a software development project, and vise-versa, without expertise in either construction or software development. There is more to successful project management than merely adhering to a set of principles.

CHAPTER FIVE

Agile Principles & Lean

Software developers created Agile as a method for undertaking their own projects efficiently and effectively. Just as Lean and Six Sigma methodologies were originally intended to benefit manufacturing, and the pioneers of these methodologies did not anticipate that they would become prominent means of managing organizations outside of manufacturing, the creators of Agile were likely unaware of the far reaching influence that they would have on project management and even organizational management.

Lean and Six Sigma focus on reducing waste and errors and maximizing efficiency in both manufacturing operations and the daily operations that occur in any organization. Whether an organization is a prominent automobile manufacturer or a corner grocery store, the principles of Lean and Six Sigma can be applied to reduce waste, increase efficiency and maximize profits. Anyone who is sufficiently familiar with Lean and or Six Sigma principles could support such a premise. Even without removing the software development components of Agile, it is evident that its principles are also compatible with Lean.

Lean & Agile

Henry Ford is credited with developing Lean in the early 20th century, though its history dates even further back than that. The Japanese manufacturer, Toyota, refined it further when Sakichi and Kiiciro Toyoda and Taiichi Ohno, after studying Henry Ford's model and methods, conceived the Toyota Production System (TPS) from the late 1940's to the 1970's. It is a system of manufacturing focused on a "Just-In-Time" philosophy: No inventory is delivered from one process to the next until the precise moment that it is needed, thus reducing the resources needed to pay for, store and maintain inventory. Lean, like Agile, was developed for a particular application, but it has come to benefit organizations far outside its original application. Each of the Agile principles can be examined and combined with Lean concepts to practice a successful project management strategy.

Agile's focus on customer satisfaction is reflected in the Lean principle of refining processes to only add value as the customer would define it. There is no value in performing any activity that does not add value to a product or service. Manufacturing a product is a set of processes that, by applying labor and work, takes raw materials and transforms them to an end user good. A simple example is making a baseball bat out of a single piece of maple. The raw material, the piece of wood, is changed into a bat by performing work on it. Turning the wood on a lathe to shape it into a bat adds value to the wood, but taking one finished bat out of the lathe and replacing it with a fresh piece of wood does not. Lean focuses on reducing the amount of time and effort required to perform operations that don't add value. If an activity does not satisfy the customer, it is wasteful and must be examined to minimize the amount of resources expended on it.

The Agile principle of accommodating change is also easily found in Lean. Toyoda made note of Henry Ford's manufacturing system and its standardization of parts and processes. Henry Ford famously said that a customer could buy an automobile painted in any color, as long as that color was black. Toyoda recognized that a system that was based solely on standardization, lacking the flexibility to accommodate change, limited the ability to satisfy the customer. Adding the ability to quickly and efficiently accommodate change, something that the Toyota Production System calls SMED (Single Minute Exchange of Die), enables greater potential for satisfying the customer at a lower cost. The Agile principle is based not only on offering options and choices to the customer, but on the realization that a customer's needs and preferences are likely to change over the course of a project, therefore the processes and tasks of the project should be designed to easily accommodate change.

The practice of meeting objectives with on-time deliverables is important in any project management methodology. It also demonstrates progress towards meeting the end goal of the project on-schedule, and thus it is an important factor in ensuring satisfied customers and users. Deliverables are what a customer pays for, even if not directly, and any activity that does not add value to deliverables should be evaluated for waste. The value stream for each deliverable should be quickly identified and mapped out in the typical Lean *Value Stream Mapping* (VSM) fashion, and kaizen events that are suspected to yield the easiest results should occur in key locations on the value stream map .

Teamwork and motivation are essential to project success. It can be difficult to motivate several people to work as a cohesive unit, particularly if some or all of them have never worked together before. Personal motivation and loyalties are often questioned and may become obstructive to meeting project goals. One of the most important factors in ensuring that team members are motivated is to make the project manager's authority visible and unquestioned with clear upper management or sponsor support. Team members should be selected who can be motivated by the singular goal of completing a successful project without becoming distracted by personal opinions about other team members. Team members who may be more concerned about how project activities may impact themselves or their own departments are often problematic and should be avoided.

Constant communication is vital to both teamwork and motivation, but it is vital to other principles as well, particularly that of sustainable progress. Metrics measure and communicate progress, and they should be visible to all team members and constantly refreshed. The practice of having a short, efficient daily meeting, often called a *stand-up meeting*, is a valuable strategy in maintaining constant communication, and it is consistent with the Agile premise that face-to-face communication is the best kind. All team members are present in these meetings. They should last no longer than 15 minutes and should be conducted according to a consistent agenda. Key Performance Indicators (KPI) or other appropriate metrics are quickly reviewed, as is the plan for the day's work on the project. The project manager leads the meeting, ensures that the meeting stays focused on useful information, and updates the project schedule accordingly. Conducting these meetings and reviewing metrics are only part of the formula; it is the evaluation and use of the information to sustain progress on a project that makes the strategy complete.

Attention to excellence requires that the terms *excellence* and *attention* to be defined. Merriam-Webster defines the word *excellent* as "superior," or "very good of its kind." The term *attention* to refers to not only an awareness of, but also the careful consideration of, and indeed the action of taking some special care of something. Paying attention to excellence is a component of the continuous improvement process that is found in Lean and Six Sigma as well as a number of Agile principles. Looking back on its Agile roots, this fundamental principle states that technical excellence and good design are key to *agility*, or the ability to react to changing environments and requirements. In project management, this principle is useful on multiple levels. Agile project management requires the ability to accommodate, and even welcome, change. Designing a mechanism for accommodating change into a project plan, or into the everyday processes that an organization completes on a regular basis, reduces the changeover time of switching from one specification or expectation to the next, which is at the foundation of the principle of accommodating change.

Of all the fundamental principles of Agile, the principle of minimal waste, or maximizing the work that is *not* done, is the principle that is most directly related to Lean. Lean defines seven individual wastes, or the Japanese term *muda*, that are present in manufacturing processes. Incidentally, it is difficult to argue that any of these wastes are not present in any other industry, as well as manufacturing. The wastes themselves, in no particular order of importance, are overproduction, defects, waiting, transportation, movement or motion, over processing and inventory. In the development of Lean and TPS, the Japanese recognized that overproduction contributed to nearly all, if not all, of the other wastes, and placed a high importance on reducing it. Specifically, the waste of overproduction was addressed by implementing a philosophy of Just-In-Time (JIT) manufacturing, that is the production or delivery of only the inventory or raw materials that are needed to complete a particular process according to that process's takt time, or the pace that is needed to support the downstream processes.

Self-organization is a concept that while not foreign to Lean, is not a primary focus of any particular Lean strategy or principle. It does, however, support Lean principles. Self-organization of project teams occurs without the direct involvement of management. It is efficient and natural. Self-organization is a key component to sustainable progress, and it does not require the use of external resources. Interestingly enough, self-organizing teams often exhibit many of the traits or principles that have already been discussed: teamwork and collaboration, self-sufficient competency, motivation, an awareness of and a priority of accomplishing the end goal of a project, and the continuity of constant communication. Each team member seamlessly and smoothly falls into his or her role with no resistance and with minimal direction or supervision. These are important components of Lean implementation strategies, and self-organization is one of the more difficult principles to maintain.

It requires an in-depth knowledge and evaluation of prospective team members' skills and abilities, and input from the project manager is extremely valuable in this regard.

The principle of continuous improvement is closely related to both excellence and sustainability. Continuous improvement should not merely be looked upon as a principle or even a practice, but a culture. It is more than making a conscious effort to do a better job. It is the constant evaluation of performance, eliciting suggestions for improvement, and acting on those suggestions before restarting the cycle. There must be a mechanism in place that fosters the culture of continuous improvement. In an attempt to portray this culture, some organizations utilize the proverbial "suggestion box," a venue for employees or members to make anonymous or named suggestions to management. Too often the suggestion box is neglected altogether while pieces of folded paper grow dusty inside it. Continuous improvement requires a strictly structured system of reflecting on the past, evaluating performance, and the presenting, evaluating and testing actionable ideas for improvement. The suggestion box method is certainly easy, but it still requires structure. Someone must be responsible for reviewing the suggestions periodically. There must be some criteria for checking the suggestions or other data that is collected against observed data, and there must be a process for evaluating suggestions and predicting the results so that a decision can be made. A record of each suggestion and any action that is taken should be made available for future reference. The suggestion box example is merely an example. The point is that a culture of continuous improvement requires structure and definition. Without structure and definition, the culture simply becomes a habit, and habits are subject to change, or cessation altogether.

CHAPTER SIX

Agile Project Management & Six Sigma

Agile methods, with their focus on customer satisfaction and the fundamental principles of metrics, sustainable progress, and attention to excellence, clearly support a culture of continuous improvement. Six Sigma does the same with a slightly more systematic and statistical approach. Six Sigma is not a system of project management, but like Lean, it is easily integrated with Agile principles to establish an efficient and successful strategy for managing projects of any nature.

Six Sigma places a high priority on customer-driven requirements. The fundamental Agile principle of minimizing waste is in agreement with the Lean principle of value added work and the Six Sigma focus on customer-driven requirements. Any effort that does not result in meeting some measurable specification that the customer is paying for is wasteful and must be reduced. Not only are both Agile and Six Sigma customer-driven, they also promote an environment of continuous effort and focus on customer satisfaction.

Six Sigma utilizes continuous statistical analysis of performance and process output. Metrics are recorded and compared to the desired results of a particular process. This concept is consistent with a number of the fundamental Agile principles like metrics, on-time deliverables, and of course minimal waste. These Six Sigma principles were originally designed for a manufacturing environment, but when they are applied to the various tasks and stages of a project, they can facilitate the success of a project. Expectations are set according to customer specifications, and the progress and outcome of each task is compared to those expectations. If expectations are not met, there must be some predetermined response that the team members take to evaluate the data and determine why expectations are not being met, and what action must be taken to correct the problem.

The term *Six Sigma* has its origins in statistics, *sigma* being a Greek symbol that represents a specific deviation from the average, or expected data. While the literal translation of the term indicates that a deviation or error rate should be limited to no more than 3.4 defects per million of output, an error rate that was intended to limit errors in a high-output manufacturing operation and may not be practical for some applications, what is important is that a maximum defect rate is calculated for any given process, and in the event that the maximum allowable defect rate is exceeded, the data and process is automatically analyzed in order to improve the output. The key to this particular strategy is to automate it. It is insufficient to periodically look into the tasks and processes of a project and to react after a problem becomes evident. You must have a process in place that guarantees the measuring and collecting of data on a specified cycle, the analysis of that data, and a predetermined action that happens if the data indicates a problem. As a simple example, team leader B, who oversees process B, which is immediately downstream of process A, is responsible for reporting the daily error rate of the process A output. The reported data is analyzed daily and is compared to the acceptable sigma for that particular process. If the data indicates that the defects are exceeding the allowable defect rate, Team Leader A and Team Leader B are automatically notified, and a meeting is held to analyze the problem and identify a solution. This example is based on a manufacturing environment, but it is easily applicable to project management in general and particularly to the software development environment for which Agile was designed. The Agile principles of teamwork, constant communication, metrics and continuous improvement should be obvious in this Six Sigma example. The data is always measured, it is always reported, and if it doesn't meet expectations, it is always acted upon. There should be no decision process involved in these three elements.

Teamwork is a core idea in both Six Sigma and Agile. Teamwork fosters and is fostered by an environment of communication and cooperation. The principles of motivation and self-organization are more easily followed when an atmosphere of teamwork is perceived. Team members should be selected and assigned in a manner that complements their knowledge and abilities. Any team member that is not immediately apparent to be a good fit should be immediately replaced. It is not uncommon for team members to experience friction, particularly after working together on often lengthy and stressful projects. This friction may be natural, and it may be just as naturally resolved without administrative action.

One key to successful teamwork on a project is the utilization of self-organizing teams. Self-organization is the result of diversity, recognizable achievement and expertise amongst team members. In selecting team members, it can be incredibly useful to use a *SWOT* analysis. A *SWOT* analysis identifies each prospective team member by his or her *Strengths*, *Weaknesses*, *Opportunities* and *Threats*. A single project manager can conduct this exercise, or it can be conducted by a senior level management or project support team. Prospective team members are identified and represented graphically by a circle that is divided into 4 parts. The known strengths and weaknesses of each prospective team member is identified and listed inside two of the circle segments. The opportunities and threats that a prospective team member can bring to the project are also likewise identified by writing them into the two remaining segments. Each prospective team member is thus analyzed and the appropriate selections and assignments are made, increasing the likelihood that the team will be self-organizing.

The Six Sigma practices of thoroughness and flexibility can be compared to the Agile principles of attention to excellence and accommodation of change. In Six Sigma, being thorough requires team members to follow the evidence, or the data, wherever it may lead, and to act upon such evidence appropriately. Being thorough also means being prepared for and accepting change. There is one strategy that can be used to promote the acceptance of change amongst project team members, and that strategy involves a mere change in terminology. The word *change* is often associated with negativity. People do not often care for change, and often prefer to stick with what they know. In the world of project management, change can mean deviating from a plan, increasing costs and decreasing profits. The term *modify*, or even *improve* often elicits an entirely different, even positive response. In both Agile and Six Sigma, change is welcomed; however, any welcomed change should be implemented in a manner that is beneficial to the end user and profitable to the project. In order to ensure that change is more often beneficial than not, the project's processes and tasks must be designed to accommodate change without disrupting downstream tasks or processes. Managing a project that can easily accommodate change is not easy; it requires a particular attitude from both the project manager and the project team members. Less important, but still important, is the use of contingency planning for tasks in which change is most likely to occur. Contingency planning should always be in writing as a part of the overall project plan. For each task, the question "What might go wrong here?" and more importantly, "What might become modified here?" should be asked. Changes and modifications to a project may be customer or end user-driven, or they may be process or team member-driven. The various team members' responses to the hypothetical questions should be identified as either customer-driven, team member-driven or process-driven, and a contingency plan should be identified for each response.

Six Sigma principles were developed as a means for predicting and measuring defects and correcting those defects in the event that they become excessive, specifically in a manufacturing environment. The history of this concept, spans hundreds of years, from the "normal curve" conceived by Carl Friedrich Gauss in the early 19th century through Walter Shewhart's early 20th century proposal of the "three sigma" variation limit, to Motorola's development of modern Six Sigma in the late 20th century, Six Sigma has proven to be a very versatile system of continuous improvement. Agile, when combined with Six Sigma, becomes much more than just a software development system. It is a self-improving system of project management that is efficient and sustainable.

CHAPTER SEVEN

Making the Most of the Methodologies

Agile has evolved from a software development system to a versatile methodology for project management. Agile does have the unique ability to evolve and to absorb or be absorbed by similar best practice methodologies in project management, as well as organizational management. Two of the most popular Agile methodologies are synergistic with Lean production.

Scrum

Scrum is one particular example of an Agile methodology that can be applied to project management, and it is also the most often used methodology in Agile software development projects.

Scrum prescribes that team members complete work on a project in regular, pre-determined cycles or iterations. The current cycle at any given time is called the Sprint. The work is divided up into a carefully prioritized backlog of tasks during a Sprint Planning Meeting. Each of the tasks represents a specific feature of a software package, which is assigned a priority according to a number of factors. Features are evaluated for user visibility and value, and the highest priorities are assigned to those features that are the most visible and valued that can be completed in one iteration, which is generally 30 days, though shorter time periods are also used when appropriate.

Once the Sprint has started, no additional features are added to it. At the end of each Sprint, a progress review takes place during which completed work is evaluated and software features are demonstrated.

A Retrospective Meeting is held, during which the team's performance is discussed and possible improvements are identified that can be implemented in the next Sprint. No developer or team that is working on any particular task or feature receives credit for any work that is completed until the task or feature is 100% complete. This entire concept is in keeping with the Agile principles of providing valuable software early and often.

Like the Lean concept of holding daily stand-up meetings with team members, and in keeping with the Agile approach to constant and face-to-face communication, Scrum utilizes 10-15 minute daily meetings in which team members discuss their accomplishments since the last meeting, what they will accomplish before the next meeting, and any obstacles to their work. It should be noted that it is customary for only the team members, which include the Scrum Manager (project manager), the developers and the quality testers to speak during the daily meeting. Upper managers may attend, but they should only observe and not interfere with the meeting. These daily meetings are essential to Agile and foster a culture of visibility, accountability and constant improvement.

Scrum does have its critics, particularly because it focuses on early deliverables rather than a product as a whole. For this reason it is often important to integrate engineering best practices, Lean practices and Six Sigma into the methodology. When properly integrated with these practices, Scrum can be a very effective methodology for project management in any of a number of product development fields from computer hardware to high-performance construction products to aircraft to automobiles.

Kanban

The Japanese engineers at Toyota conceived the Kanban concept while they were developing the TPS system of Lean. Lean utilizes the JIT philosophy, that of not producing, or taking delivery of, any inventory that is not immediately needed by a downstream process. The kanban was a visible signal, originally a color-coded card, that was transmitted by a particular process when it was in need of inventory replenishment. Kanbans can occur in stages that are customized to any particular industry or process. A yellow kanban can signify that only one week's worth of inventory is on hand, an orange to signify a day's worth and a red to signify immediate need. Depending on the lead-time for new inventory, and the takt or cycle time for a process, the kanban signals can be adjusted appropriately. If inventory replenishment can occur within minutes or even hours, a red kanban may be all that is needed. If it takes days or weeks to replenish inventory, a red and a yellow card may be needed: the yellow to signal purchasing to order new inventory, and a red to signal an upstream process to deliver the inventory when it is needed. The purpose of the Kanban system is to reduce the wastes of inventory and waiting and to ensure that each process receives precisely what it needs precisely when it is needed.

Kanban's role is similar in the Agile and Lean methodologies. Similar to Scrum, the work is completed according to a carefully prioritized backlog. The difference between the two methodologies is that Scrum prescribes that the work be completed in cycles or Sprints without limiting the workload - remember that Sprints can last up to 30 days - while Kanban prescribes that no one worker or process should be given a workload that can't be completed to support continuous motion or progress. Each team or process is supplied with precisely the workload that is needed to supply the downstream teams or processes with enough work to keep up with the takt time. Kanban limits the work that is in progress (WIP) at any given time, which is consistent with Agile's principle of minimal waste. The Kanban Agile methodology focuses on communication between processes with the integration of calculated cycle times and lead times.

Extreme Programming

Extreme Programming (XP) is an Agile methodology that is primarily focused on releasing software frequently in response to changing or evolving customer requirements. XP is solely a system of software development, but it does incorporate some Lean ideas. The XP practice avoids programming features that are not immediately needed, which is similar to the Kanban methodology and it is certainly Lean. XP prescribes four basic activities that occur throughout the software development processes of a project.

Coding is the subject of primary attention in XP, and it is the first of the four basic activities. Coding is the basis of accomplishing any programming goal, so XP programmers must place a priority on generating code as early in the development process as possible. XP also incorporates certain aspects of Six Sigma in the *automated testing* of all code, which is consistent with the built-in quality in Lean and Six Sigma. By performing testing in small increments, waste is eliminated by reducing the amount of time that each process is waiting on the deliverables. Testing the finished code from an upstream process ensures that defects are identified immediately rather than later, when revisions to code can be more difficult and time consuming. *Listening* is another of the four basic activities. XP places a high priority on constant customer involvement and communication so that expectations are always visible and clear. XP programmers must be excellent listeners in order to meet customer expectations. It may seem counterintuitive that *designing* is the last of the four activities, but given the high priority on getting code written so it can be tested and given to the customer for feedback, it is not surprising that the designing activity is placed where it is. As backwards as this process seems, when code is generated and tested daily as intended, the cycle is very short. One of the basic ideas of XP is that without code there is nothing, therefore coding must come first.

Lean Software Development

Lean software development is an Agile methodology that is, of course, named after Toyota's Lean Manufacturing. Its principles give developers a set of tools that enable them to design and build the specific processes that they need for their software development projects. Lean manufacturing places a high value on eliminating waste. Lean software development accomplishes this by eliminating wasted time and steps and by automating testing and eliminating useless or unused code. Feedback loops decrease learning cycle time and testing cycle time, further reducing waste.

There is also an emphasis on delaying the decision-making process as long as possible. By waiting to make a decision, more knowledge, information or data is accumulated, which makes the decision more informed. Opposite the delayed decision-making is the accelerated delivery. Like XP, Lean development strives to deliver something as soon as possible so that it can be tested and evaluated by the customer, who then provides the feedback that is needed in order to improve the product. Teamwork is essential, and Lean development empowers teams by assigning well-qualified team members and letting them do their respective jobs. Quality is built into both the team and the code in order to ensure that the product meets expectations from the developers to the end user. A complete picture of the project is kept within view, so that collaboration between team members and software features or components can be more easily facilitated.

The critics of Agile often point out that its principles, or any of its methodologies, are insufficient to be considered an effective methodology of project management, particularly outside the world of software development. Perhaps a brief manifesto and a list of principles are insufficient for the complete management of software development projects from start to finish while meeting both the customer or user's requirements and those of the organization. However, Agile is well suited for integration with Lean principles as in the above methodologies, and they are certainly well-suited for development projects.

CHAPTER EIGHT

Agile in Action : Departing from Waterfall

Agile, along with its many spin-off project management methodologies such as Scrum and Lean, came into its own during the first decade of the 21st century. The prevailing pre-Agile approach to project management is commonly known as the "Waterfall" method. Distinctions between Agile and Waterfall are many. On several fronts, the Agile approach represents a clear and direct departure from Waterfall. The Waterfall approach is comparable to the methods used in a large-scale construction project. Estimates are established early on for the project budget and timeline. The product (a structure or building) must be completed before it is useable. Opportunities for change are limited considering once the foundation and build style is established, it's very difficult to retroactively refit the product with a different style.

In its departure from Waterfall, Agile has identified the unique opportunities for versatility within the software development mechanism. Agile produces short, targeted iterative bursts of work that are immediately useable and systematically reviewed. The Waterfall process relied on strict specialization and segregation of various skills. Much like a carpenter wouldn't try and weld, a software tester following the Waterfall method wouldn't contribute to coding or artistic design. Agile, by contrast, encourages cross-functional teams and cross-functional processes, such as Test Driven Development (TDD) and Pair Programming, which we'll examine in Chapter 9.

Syneto

Transitioning out of Waterfall and into Agile isn't always a quick and simple process. In 2014, Patkós Csaba, a programmer at a software firm in Romania called Syneto, published an account of his company's journey through the Waterfall process and into Agile. Csaba describes the work environment before Waterfall as chaotic. The company would continually exceed their budgets and fall behind schedule on their product releases. The company responded immediately to any and all client demands, even if it meant turbulent interruptions and redirections in workflow. "There was little documentation, like in Agile... but there was nothing agile about our process."

Csaba reports that the company's development process became more organized in 2008 when it adopted a Waterfall approach. With Waterfall, the team at least had a process to follow, an alternative to pure chaos, but as Csaba notes, the process was so clunky that "it probably introduced more bugs and delays than the chaos before it." Csaba recounts one telling incident that transpired while Syneto was developing a notification feature for its legacy project, the Unified Threat Management (UTM) appliance. Aiming to improve development speed and product reliability, the project manager secluded himself in a separate office for two days and came up with an elaborate architecture for the new feature. When the project manager emerged from hiding he discovered that in just a half-day the team had produced a working one-page script for the feature.

When these types of senseless communication failures, along with bugs and delays, became unbearable, the company responded by doubling down on Waterfall. Documents were written about how to write other documents. Then they planned everything, including detailed class specifications, with pieces of code and algorithms. Functionalities and test scenarios were also detailed in lengthy documents. The process concentrated so much on implementation details, that anybody, after reading such a document, should have been able to implement the solution. The details were amazing. Unfortunately, the additional planning requirements did little to improve the quality of the product and the processes. Delays grew even longer. Release cycles ballooned out to nine months. And bugs were more prevalent than ever. Given the substantial amount of time and energy that organizations like Syneto put into the Waterfall process, we're left to wonder why this method so often fails. The answer to the question, simply put, is Waterfall's lack of *agility*. The business universe is volatile, and customer strategies and needs continually shift. Add that to the fast-evolving, ever dynamic universe of software design and implementation, and you're left with a predicament in which versatility (or *agility*) is of critical importance. In many ways the Agile framework was designed in response to the flaws of the once dominant Waterfall system.

After Syneto's failed implementation of Waterfall framework, the company found itself on the brink of financial failure. In the latter months of 2009 one of Mr. Csaba's managers got ahold of Kent Beck's *Extreme Programming Explained* and Andrew Hunt's T*he Pragmatic Programmer*. In characteristic self-organizing fashion, Agile philosophy began to leak into the ailing enterprise by way of literature and experimentation. By 2010, Syneto's coders discovered unit testing. As Csaba reports, "I got hooked on the idea of automated testing immediately. Before this moment in my career, I had not even heard about programs testing programs."

Agile implementation is a process of self-discovery at the *team level*. With a host of sub-philosophies and frameworks within the Agile family, various organizations may realize Agile's benefits in ways meaningful and fitting to their specific needs. We'll return shortly to Syneto's unique journey into Agile, but first let's take a look at one other case study.

Dutch Railways

Dutch Railways was in search of a new information system to communicate travel information to their 1.2 million daily customers. Their current system relied too heavily on manual oversight, and they wanted something with more automation. Though the requirements for such a system may have seemed very straightforward – alert people to scheduling information, changes, delays, etc. – the realities of the project proved challenging and cumbersome, as should have been anticipated given the marvelous scale of the project. The first attempt to build this system, which would be known as "PUB" (short for Publish), relied on the Waterfall framework. Dutch Railways hired an IT vendor and provided an exhaustive and detailed list of specifications for the project. The result was disaster. The vendor was unable to produce a working system, and after three years the project was scrapped entirely.

The authors of the case study, Van Vliet and Marco Mulder, were employees of the company that was hired to rebuild PUB from the ground up. The new company decided to pursue the project using Scrum, but before jumping into their first Release Planning Meeting, they wanted to ensure that they were optimally prepared to take on a project of such vast scope. A "kick off meeting" was set up with an assigned project manager, an architect, and a Scrum Master. This meeting's principle order of business was the careful selection of an appropriate Product Owner. The group eventually nominated two business analysts who had been privy to the PUB system's previous development efforts. Since these analysts didn't have any real experience with Scrum, the Scrum Master helped them convert the previous effort's requirement list into User Stories that would form the new project's first Product Backlog.

The conversion process from Waterfall to Scrum proceeded relatively smoothly for Dutch Railways. The new team was able to make the most of the resources left over in the wake of the first failed 3-year effort. Nonetheless, as was the case with Syneto, failure to adopt Scrum from the onset of the project contributed to massive waste and project delays.

Syneto, however, a smaller company in a less developed part of the world, pieced together its Agile journey from the ground up. Everyone, even the managers, was new to Agile. During Syneto's early adoption of Agile, Csaba recounts his manager, Flavius, arriving an hour late: "This was very unusual since he was always one hour early every day. But there was a reason for all of this. We didn't know what yet, but there was." Flavius had spent the morning gathering materials for what would be Syneto's first ever Scrum planning board. It began very simply, with sticky notes labeled with tasks that needed doing and different columns such as "Development" and "Done" to denote the status of the tasks. At this point in time there were no meetings, just some semblance of collective organization introduced into the work environment.

Over the following weeks, the board ended up doing little to alter the processes of the employees. There was still a lot of detailed front-end planning for projects, and results continued to be less than ideal. Csaba notes that keeping up with the board did, over time, contribute to a healthy team psychology,

> ***"We started to believe that what we were doing was headed in the right direction. We started to believe we were writing software in a more organized way and that it would lead to better stability and more predictable releases."***

The next Agile feature to be introduced to the Syneto environment was Retrospective Meetings. They began as very informal venues for weekly reflection. Over time, Flavius incorporated more Agile elements into the Retrospective meetings such as writing columns on a whiteboard for: Good, Bad, and Actions to Take. Every team member was required to contribute a minimum of three ideas to each column.

The concept of the Sprint was introduced next. The team opted for short Sprints, usually one week at a time. Csaba reports that the

Sprints promoted prioritization and discipline, but most importantly, communication. Sprint-specific objectives added a new layer of urgency to the communication flow and ended up challenging Csaba's comfort level. "Talking for the first time in front of the whole team induced a certain amount of anxiety. Fortunately we all learned to overcome it."

Syneto continued to introduce aspects of Agile to its work environment item-by-item, week-by-week. Included among them were the methods of Scrum, Lean, and Kanban. When Csaba published the case study, he reported a new problem. The team had become so accustomed to using Agile methods that the formal documentation and meeting schedules began to disappear from the routines of Syneto's personnel. "We still thought about the practices actively. We still stopped for a few seconds from time to time to consider the rules and decide the next steps to take. And we managed quite well…Most of our procedures disappeared. They morphed into our culture. They shaped us and the way we act reflexively, without thinking." Csaba goes on to discuss the problem of acclimating new personnel to Agile methodology in the absence of a formal, visible process. He concludes his report declaring that a meeting had been held to discuss the issue of visible Agile procedures, and that a decision was made to "analyze" and "dissect" the culture at Syneto in order to reverse-engineer their self-evident progress back into written procedure.

CHAPTER NINE

Agile in Action : Processes & Development

Test Driven Development (TDD) is one of Agile's preferred methods when it comes to coding. Within the Agile framework the process of TDD begins with a Development Team assessing a new User Story. Before work begins to solve the problem expressed by the User Story, a test is set up that is built to fail unless the User Story has been resolved. The test is run before any work begins and, of course, fails. New code, aimed at resolving the User Story, is written and inserted into the developing program. The test is run again, presumably returning a successful result. Afterwards, a series of tests are run, most of which, like the current test, were originally built to test a User Story's resolution. These subsequent tests are to assure that the most recently added code does not compromise or corrupt the execution of previously written code. If any of the tests in the series fail, the problem is investigated, the code is altered as needed, and the tests are all repeated until all tests report back with a "green" (passing) result. The most recent test, designed to test the current User Story, is then added to the regression suite. The User Story is resolved, and the Development Team is free to move on to the next User Story or other order of business.

Pair Programming is also a prized Agile tactic. Pair Programming is a practice in which two members of a development team work on a single workstation. One person constructs code while the other watches, offers input, and double checks the work. While Pair Programming won't always result in more code being written, it will usually result in fewer errors and better standardized coding output overall. While rescuing their PUB system (see Chapter 8), Dutch Railways employed

Pair Programming extensively.

An interesting example of both of these practices in action comes from a case study called "Tearing Down the Walls," authored by Stephanie Savoia. In "Tearing Down the Walls," Savoia explains how her company, Marchex, used TDD and Pair Programming (also known as "Pairing") to improve an encumbered Quality Assurance (QA) regimen.

Marchex had long been utilizing a Waterfall approach to software development, replete with highly detailed front-end reports. To start things off, the business analysts would produce a Functional Specification Document (FSD). The FSD gave a rundown of exactly what Marchex needed and why. Using the FSD, the development team responded by producing an Outline Systems Design (OSD) document, which was essentially a proposal for the project, how it could be done, timelines, etc. From there, the Quality Assurance (QA) team used both the FSD and the OSD to write a test plan. If revisionary meetings transpired that changed the contents of the FSD or OSD, as they almost always did, then the QA team would be responsible for revising the test plan accordingly. Savoia describes the process in its entirety as "exhausting."

The decision to "go Agile" was made in early 2010, though employment of Agile methods was far from uniform across various sectors of the company. Some teams within the company adopted a halfhearted approach to Agile deployment that Savoia refers to as "Agile-Fall." Savoia identifies the continued disconnect between coding and the testing as a specific problem point. Even before Agile, the company was having trouble fostering cooperation between development teams and QA. Part of the problem was geographical; QA was housed in a separate office, a separate building even, on the opposite side of the block. During its Agile implementation, Marchex leased new office space hoping that QA and the development teams might enjoy more fruitful collaboration if placed in closer proximity to one another, but as Savoia reports, the mental divide between the two departments was already well entrenched. "People were still not partnering and were cutting themselves off to conversations behind their cube walls. Think of a child closing their eyes and saying, 'You can't see me.' It's pretty much how a few people were behaving."

The QA-Dev Détente

At the root of the divide between QA and the developer teams, also known as "Devs," was fear. The Devs didn't want to work with QA because they weren't in a hurry to learn testing procedures and thereby incur larger workloads for themselves. QA in turn feared that if the developers began coding, then QA was in danger of ceding away a dangerous amount of their unique utility.

The introduction of Test-Driven Development (TDD) ultimately forced the long-overdue collaboration between the Devs and QA. It would be impossible for the Devs to follow the coding procedure proscribed by TDD if they did not learn how to test.

Many elements of the Agile framework were already in place at this time. Once it became apparent that the Devs and QA teams would have no choice but to work alongside one another, resources were consolidated, not for the sake of scarcity, but for efficiency. The QA and Devs began to share the same Scrum board. Rather than having two separate retrospective meetings, the QA and Dev retrospectives were combined into one. After fears were abated, it became clear how the QA team's influence on the front-end of the development process could prove useful. QA helped the Dev team anticipate and avoid programming vulnerabilities that would likely manifest at some point in the future if the Dev team didn't heed QA's advice. Management was also restructured, which inevitably did cause some anxiety. QA managers were absorbed into the Dev team as Software Developers in Test (SDETs) or Sr. QA and Technical Program Managers. Many QA engineers were asked to work regularly alongside the Dev team, which created high anxiety. These engineers had become accustomed to the formulaic processes they were in charge of implementing after the Dev team completed work. Being involved on the front end of product development intimidated them. Many in engineering transferred to different departments. One individual quit. Another engineer became so proficient with front-end processes that she ended up becoming a developer.

The QA Exodus

Many QA engineers simply remained QA engineers with greatly expanded roles. In addition to helping to develop and catalog tests that would propel the TDD process, QA team members also became involved in end-user interviews. The company had an elaborate system in place to solicit feedback from its products' end users. The process involved structured interviews, record keeping, and advocacy for the customer's stated needs during the development planning process. The QA engineers became a part of this process and assisted the Dev team to create meaningful User Stories and products with better workflow and usage scenarios.

Over the course of this transition in work detail, the formal ratio of QA personnel to Dev personnel shifted. Before Agile was in full swing, Savoia's team was composed of 15 Devs and nine QAs. After six rigorous months of integrating Agile, the ratio was 13 Devs and one QA. The Agile adoption process "exposed team members who could keep an open mind... and those who couldn't."

In addition to Savoia's team, there were five other teams operating in Marchex at that time. Some of them had QAs and others did not. The teams without QAs shared an "uber QA lead that advocates for the users, advises the developers when they have questions and shadows them when they are validating their code in the testing environment."

Pair Programming

Savoia also notes her participation in a highly productive pairing relationship with members of the Dev team. Savoia belonged to the QA team, the class of employee that, before Marchex decided to adopt Agile, was only responsible for back-end testing. Fortunately for Savoia, she was among those who adapted to and grew within the new system. One of her roles was to engage in Pair Programming with Dev team members. She helped design appropriate unit tests that would spur along TDD efforts. She would also review User Stories and acceptance criteria prior to the onset of coding.

Before working under Agile, Savoia had tested code for 10 years and was quite familiar with the traditional Waterfall process, "I would have done the validation, found bugs, written bug reports, waited for the corrected code, re-validated the data and repeated until I was comfortable with the build and the data." The tedium of this process stands in contrast to Savoia's description of her post-Agile routine, "I was right there sitting with the developer and we were validating the data together. We were coding and testing and we were creating as we went."

Savoia reports that, thanks to effective Pair Programming, they cut months off production timelines. Such an account is interesting considering the common belief that Pair Programming takes longer than programming by a single party. But when the Pair Programming tactic is evaluated within the context of the Marchex environment at that time, with a flood of QA testing refugees struggling to regain their footing within the organization, it makes sense that the resourceful ones would find their way into successful Pair Programming relationships with Dev team members.

The deployment of TDD and Pair Programming are mainstays in Agile precisely because of the opportunities they present for integration, process streamlining, and higher-quality product output. The lesson to be learned from the Marchex study is that adopting the Agile framework, just like any major modification to an organization's processes, can present unique challenges, especially when traditional roles get scrambled up. Part of being successful with Agile is knowing when and how to roll out its various key components. Marchex was wise to institute Test Driven Development after the Dev and QA teams reached a communication détente. The case study's author, Stephanie Savoia, showed similar wisdom when she lent her talents to the Dev team as a Pair Programmer.

CHAPTER TEN

Evolving & Customizing Agile Metrics

The Marchex study illustrated that tactical and timely deployment of Agile framework components was ever evolving and responsive to the needs the company. When a company is going through a significant transition—such as the transition from Waterfall to Agile—then it is to be expected that such sudden urgent needs can and will arise. Another need for agility within Agile comes in the formulation and implementation of various metrics used to measure product development timelines, team performance, and customer satisfaction. Daniel Vacanti of Corporate Kanban, Inc. and Bennet Vallet of Siemens Health Services authored a 2014 case study detailing how traditional Agile metrics, such as Story Points and Velocity, were replaced with actionable flow metrics such as Work In Progress, Cycle Time, and Throughput. The end result of this modification to the Agile framework led to a 42% reduction in turnover time and improved overall operational efficiency.

Siemen HS's Bold and Resolute Adoption of Agile

Unlike the case studies discussed in previous chapters, Siemens' implementation of Agile wasn't slow and tentative. When they decided to go Agile, they did so with guns blazing, Siemens Health Services is a global provider of healthcare information systems. They service hospitals and large physician group practices. Siemens HS has a separate branch devoted entirely to software and hardware development. It's called Product Lifestyle Management (PLM). PLM consists of fifty teams, primarily headquartered in Malvern, Pennsylvania, but with auxiliary development resources in India and Europe.

Central to the Siemen HS business model is the rapid development of new products— leveraging the newest technology—to leapfrog competing systems that, though they may be more mature, are not reflections of the best product possible. Siemens invested heavily in the transition, securing the most prominent experts and coaches in the community to help them along. By September 2011, Siemen's Agile process was "mature," having incorporated most all Scrum and Extreme Programming (XP) practices.

The Need for Greater Predictability

The results of thorough Agile implementation at Siemens were good but not perfect. Siemens recognized vast improvement in the collaboration among and within teams, improved customer functionality, and improved code quality and speed. Unfortunately, however, there were certain aspects of Siemens' business objectives that Agile did little to improve. Because Siemens serves the healthcare industry, it's subject to a host of regulations imposed by the Food and Drug Administration (FDA), International Standards Organization (IS), and Sarbanes-Oxley. These regulations ensure auditability, patient safety, and proper reporting practices. The result of these regulatory concerns is a need for clear definition and more certainty in product development timelines.

As we know, Agile promotes self-regulating systems that emphasize prioritization, cross-functional collaboration, and flexibility. Agile in turn de-emphasizes strict timelines and ironclad front-end planning. As Vacanti and Vallet note:

> *"Our internal decision checkpoints and quality gates required firm commitments. Our Commitment to customers, internal stakeholder expectations and revenue forecasts required release scope and delivery forecasts that carry a very high premium for delay."*

The first Agile metric that began giving the Siemen HS developers trouble was the Velocity rating, which Vacanti defines quite simply as the "number of points completed in a Sprint." A look behind the scenes revealed that even though a good number of stories were being completed in each Sprint on average, there were way too many outstanding features that sat on the Backlog for weeks or months at a time without resolution. Teams would be waiting for other teams to complete dependency items, and rather than assign a deadline, they would simply create more Stories to be resolved in the next Sprint so they could claim the points. The end result was a lack of real predictability for certain tasks and projects. Considered within the context of Siemen HS's need for predictable, timely output, the Velocity metric ultimately was causing more harm than good.

Introducing Kanban

Siemens HS had a lot invested in Agile and expected results. In November of 2011, Siemens HS executive management put together a team of director-level managers for the purpose of process improvement in the PLM organization. The team reviewed the existing process using the "Lean" perspective and came to the conclusion that the problems Siemens HS was facing were systemic ones, namely that the company had a tendency to plan and execute large feature releases, which allowed larger than usual batch sizes. Too much material was getting jammed up in systemic cues. Employees were working overtime and on weekends without shortening release completion dates.

Kanban was seen as a means of enforcing Lean standards while still maintaining Agile methodology. Kanban provides an opportunity for new metrics such as Work in Progress, Cycle Time, and Throughput. Such metrics were perceived by the director-level managers as being more tangible, actionable and more easily understood by corporate stakeholders.

A massive rollout of Kanban ensued from Malvern, PA to Kolkata, India. Large monitors were placed in all team rooms so everyone's progress could be monitored globally across the company. The first product release using Kanban began in April 2012 and was completed by December of the same year. Cycle Time looked predictable, and defects were lower than expected. The company began their second release using Kanban in March 2013, incorporating lessons from the first release. The results of the second release were even better than the first.

The Metric Shift & Little's Law

Vacanti credits the success of the Kanban approach to the change in the key metrics. Whereas teams could easily manipulate Velocity to make themselves look good in the aftermath of a sprint or project, the Throughput metric, as it was defined by Work In Progress (WIP) and Cycle Time, was more foolproof, "With Velocity, a team measures story points per iteration. With Throughput a team simply counts the number of work items complete per arbitrary unit of time. That unit could be days, week, months—or even iterations."

These three new metrics are interrelated and can be expressed and, most importantly, acted upon using Little's Law, which states that Average Work in Progress over Average Throughput equals Average Cycle Time.

The lesson of the Siemens HS example is that some Agile sub-frameworks, such as Scrum, may not always come equipped with the specific metrics needed for the business purposes of certain organizations, either because of size, goals, or problem-solving approach. However, because a multitude of options are available in the Agile family: Scrum, Kanban, Lean, etc., there's usually a way for organizations to maintain the benefits of the Agile framework while finding and customizing the metrics they need.

Agile has evolved from a software development system to a versatile methodology for project management. Agile does have the unique ability to evolve and to absorb or be absorbed by similar best practice methodologies in project management, as well as organizational management. Two of the most popular Agile methodologies are synergistic with Lean production.

Scrum

Scrum is one particular example of an Agile methodology that can be applied to project management, and it is also the most often used methodology in Agile software development projects.

Scrum prescribes that team members complete work on a project in regular, pre-determined cycles or iterations. The current cycle at any given time is called the Sprint. The work is divided up into a carefully prioritized backlog of tasks during a Sprint Planning Meeting. Each of the tasks represents a specific feature of a software package, which is assigned a priority according to a number of factors. Features are evaluated for user visibility and value, and the highest priorities are assigned to those features that are the most visible and valued that can be completed in one iteration, which is generally 30 days, though shorter time periods are also used when appropriate.

Once the Sprint has started, no additional features are added to it. At the end of each Sprint, a progress review takes place during which completed work is evaluated and software features are demonstrated. A Retrospective Meeting is held, during which the team's performance is discussed and possible improvements are identified that can be implemented in the next Sprint. No developer or team that is working on any particular task or feature receives credit for any work that is completed until the task or feature is 100% complete. This entire concept is in keeping with the Agile principles of providing valuable software early and often.

Like the Lean concept of holding daily stand-up meetings with team members, and in keeping with the Agile approach to constant and face-to-face communication, Scrum utilizes 10-15 minute daily meetings in which team members discuss their accomplishments since the last meeting, what they will accomplish before the next meeting, and any obstacles to their work. Upper managers may attend, but they should only observe and not interfere with the meeting. These daily meetings are essential to Agile and foster a culture of visibility, accountability and constant improvement.

Scrum does have its critics, particularly because it focuses on early deliverables rather than a product as a whole. For this reason it is often important to integrate engineering best practices, Lean practices and Six Sigma into the methodology. When properly integrated with these practices, Scrum can be a very effective methodology for project management in any of a number of product development fields from computer hardware to high-performance construction products to aircraft to automobiles.

Kanban

The Japanese engineers at Toyota conceived the Kanban concept while they were developing the TPS system of Lean. Lean utilizes the JIT philosophy, that of not producing, or taking delivery of, any inventory that is not immediately needed by a downstream process. The kanban was a visible signal, originally a color-coded card, that was transmitted by a particular process when it was in need of inventory replenishment. Kanbans can occur in stages that are customized to any particular industry or process. A yellow kanban can signify that only one week's worth of inventory is on hand, an orange to signify a day's worth and a red to signify immediate need. Depending on the lead-time for new inventory, and the takt or cycle time for a process, the kanban signals can be adjusted appropriately. If inventory replenishment can occur within minutes or even hours, a red kanban may be all that is needed. If it takes days or weeks to replenish inventory, a red and a yellow card may be needed: the yellow to signal purchasing to order new inventory, and a red to signal an upstream process to deliver the inventory when it is needed. The purpose of the Kanban system is to reduce the wastes of inventory and waiting and to ensure that each process receives precisely what it needs precisely when it is needed.

Kanban's role is similar in the Agile and Lean methodologies. Similar to Scrum, the work is completed according to a carefully prioritized backlog. The difference between the two methodologies is that Scrum prescribes that the work be completed in cycles or Sprints without limiting the workload - remember that Sprints can last up to 30 days - while Kanban prescribes that no one worker or process should be given a workload that can't be completed to support continuous motion or progress. Each team or process is supplied with precisely the workload that is needed to supply the downstream teams or processes with enough work to keep up with the takt time. Kanban limits the work that is in progress (WIP) at any given time, which is consistent with Agile's principle of minimal waste. The Kanban Agile methodology focuses on communication between processes with the integration of calculated cycle times and lead times.

Extreme Programming

Extreme Programming (XP) is an Agile methodology that is primarily focused on releasing software frequently in response to changing or evolving customer requirements. XP is solely a system of software development, but it does incorporate some Lean ideas. The XP practice avoids programming features that are not immediately needed, which is similar to the Kanban methodology and it is certainly Lean. XP prescribes four basic activities that occur throughout the software development processes of a project.

Coding is the subject of primary attention in XP, and it is the first of the four basic activities. Coding is the basis of accomplishing any programming goal, so XP programmers must place a priority on generating code as early in the development process as possible. XP also incorporates certain aspects of Six Sigma in the *automated testing* of all code, which is consistent with the built-in quality in Lean and Six Sigma. By performing testing in small increments, waste is eliminated by reducing the amount of time that each process is waiting on the deliverables. Testing the finished code from an upstream process ensures that defects are identified immediately rather than later, when revisions to code can be more difficult and time consuming. *Listening* is another of the four basic activities. XP places a high priority on constant customer involvement and communication so that expectations are always visible and clear. XP programmers must be excellent listeners in order to meet customer expectations. It may seem counterintuitive that *designing* is the last of the four activities, but given the high priority on getting code written so it can be tested and given to the customer for feedback, it is not surprising that the designing activity is placed where it is. As backwards as this process seems, when code is generated and tested daily as intended, the cycle is very short. One of the basic ideas of XP is that without code there is nothing, therefore coding must come first.

Lean Software Development

Lean software development is an Agile methodology that is, of course, named after Toyota's Lean Manufacturing. Its principles give developers a set of tools that enable them to design and build the specific processes that they need for their software development projects.

Lean manufacturing places a high value on eliminating waste. Lean software development accomplishes this by eliminating wasted time and steps and by automating testing and eliminating useless or unused code. Feedback loops decrease learning cycle time and testing cycle time, further reducing waste. There is also an emphasis on delaying the decision-making process as long as possible. By waiting to make a decision, more knowledge, information or data is accumulated, which makes the decision more informed. Opposite the delayed decision-making is the accelerated delivery. Like XP, Lean development strives to deliver something as soon as possible so that it can be tested and evaluated by the customer, who then provides the feedback that is needed in order to improve the product.

Teamwork is essential, and Lean development empowers teams by assigning well-qualified team members and letting them do their respective jobs. Quality is built into both the team and the code in order to ensure that the product meets expectations from the developers to the end user. A complete picture of the project is kept within view, so that collaboration between team members and software features or components can be more easily facilitated.

The critics of Agile often point out that its principles, or any of its methodologies, are insufficient to be considered an effective methodology of project management, particularly outside the world of software development. Perhaps a brief manifesto and a list of principles are insufficient for the complete management of software development projects from start to finish while meeting both the customer or user's requirements and those of the organization. However, Agile is well suited for integration with Lean principles as in the above methodologies, and they are certainly well-suited for development projects.

CONCLUSION

Additional Resources

Despite a lack of institutional literature on Agile, there are a number of educational resources online. The website **http://agilemanifesto.org** displays the manifesto that was developed by the original 17 software developers that devised the system itself. The website also lists 12 principles of Agile software as well as a brief history of the system. Perhaps the most useful resource on the website is a link that leads to a brief bibliography and history of each of the original authors of the manifesto. By following that link, a list of the authors is accessible, each with his or her own link. A number of the authors have written extensively about either Agile or a number of other software development subjects.

Jim Highsmith, one of the founders of Agile and co-author of the Agile Manifesto, can be found through the Jim Highsmith link on the Agile Manifesto site.

He has authored :

- Agile Project Management: Creating Innovative Products (Addison-Wesley 2009),
- Agile Software Development Ecosystems (Addison-Wesley, 2002),
- Adaptive Software Development: A Collaborative Approach to Managing Complex Systems (Dorset House, 2000)

College courses and certificate programs that offer education and training in Agile project management are also widely available at a number of high profile institutions. University of California, Los Angeles, University of California, Berkeley, Miami University and many others offer basic and advanced courses in Agile, Agile Project Management and Agile Lean Six Sigma. University of California, Irvine offers an online certificate program called Agile Project Management. The program is designed for working professionals who already have a familiarity with agile and wish to expand their knowledge to industry-specific applications.

In the rapidly evolving world of software development, it is not likely that any single methodology will last with indefinite support from industry leaders. The software needs of users today are very different than they werein 2001 when Agile was developed. They will be very different ten years from now, and are very likely to change even more as information and communication technology evolves to meet the user needs. Software development techniques will be forced to evolve along with the users and the technology. Fortunately, Agile has been a sustainable self-improving methodology and true to its name, for in the future it is agility and the ability to stay lightweight and constantly accommodating to change that will result in the most successful software development.

Agile has been criticized as being developer-centric in spite of its focus on the customer or end user. Critics often cite Agile's primary focus on the early delivery of working software as a measurement of success, stating that this principle leads to errors in the product as programmers rush to develop software. These critics overlook the fact that Agile specifies that such software be "valuable." By implementing Lean and Six Sigma strategies, the outcome or result of any Agile project is far more likely to be valuable to the end user. In addition, the culture of constant improvement that is inherent to both Lean and Six Sigma methodologies, when combined with Agile, will continue to facilitate its evolution to match the users' needs.

ABOUT CLYDEBANK BUSINESS

ClydeBank Business is a division of the multimedia-publishing firm ClydeBank Media LLC. ClydeBank Media's goal is to provide affordable, accessible information to a global market through different forms of media such as eBooks, paperback books and audio books. Company divisions are based on subject matter, each consisting of a dedicated team of researchers, writers, editors and designers.

The Business division of ClydeBank Media is composed of contributors who are experts in their given disciplines. Contributors originate from diverse areas of the world to guarantee the presented information fosters a global perspective.

Contributors have multiple years of experience in successfully starting and operating online and offline businesses, marketing and sales, economics, management methodology and systems, business consulting, manufacturing efficiency and many other areas of discipline.

For more information, please visit us at :
www.clydebankmedia.com
or contact us at :
info@clydebankmedia.com

MORE BY CLYDEBANK BUSINESS

Scrum QuickStart Guide
A Simplified Beginners Guide To Mastering Scrum
Visit : bit.ly/scrumguide1

Agile Project Management Quickstart Guide
A Simplified Beginners Guide To Agile Project Management
Visit : bit.ly/agile_quickstart

Agile Project Management & Scrum Box Set
Agile Project Management QuickStart Guide
& Scrum QuickStart Guide
Visit : bit.ly/agileprojectmana

Lean Six Sigma QuickStart Guide
A Simplified Beginners Guide To Lean Six Sigma
Visit : bit.ly/lean-sixsigma

3D Printing Business
How To Get Rich From Home With 3D Printing
Visit : bit.ly/3dprinting_rich

Project Management For Beginners
Proven Project Management Methods To
Complete Projects With Time & Money To Spare
Visit : bit.ly/project_success

Copywriting Mastery
Exactly How To Become A Professional Copywriting Expert
& Create Content That Gets Attention & Sells
Visit : bit.ly/CopywritingMastery

Business Plan Writing Guide
How To Write A Successful & Sustainable
Business Plan in Under 3 Hours
Visit : bit.ly/businessplanwriting

eBay Business For Beginners
Exactly How I Make A Six Figure Income With My eBay
Business And Why It Is Easier Than You Think
Visit : bit.ly/ebay_rich

Etsy Business For Beginners
How To Build & Promote A Profitable Etsy Business
Visit : bit.ly/etsy_business

Etsy & eBay Business Box Set
Etsy Business For Beginners & eBay Business For Beginners
Visit : bit.ly/ebay_etsy

CPSIA information can be obtained at www.ICGtesting.com
Printed in the USA
LVOW04s0332270715

447750LV00029B/720/P

9 780996 366748